Basketball's Zone Presses: A Complete Coaching Guide

BURRALL PAYE

Parker Publishing Company, Inc.
West Nyack, New York

Library of Congress Cataloging in Publication Data

Paye, Burrall
  Basketball's zone presses.

  Includes index.
  1. Basketball—Defense.   2. Basketball—Coaching.
I. Title.
GV888.P37 1983   796.32′32   83-13186
ISBN 0-13-069237-9

To
Jack Leach
a hard taskmaster, a special friend, and my editor

Also by the author

Complete Coaching Guide to Basketball's Match-Up Zone
The Winning Power of Pressure Defense in Basketball
Coaching the Full-Court Man-to-Man Press
Secrets of the Passing-Dribbling Game Offense

How This Book Will Help You Develop Your Zone Press Defenses

Zone presses can create chaos and spread fear to even the best drilled offensive squads. Their infinite trapping situations, their diversified gap shootings, their unlimited stunts, and their endless points of initial and secondary pressure confuse foes, leading many proponents from the jaws of defeat to the ecstasy of victory. These same maneuvers have enabled promoters of the zone presses to run away with victory in games that otherwise would have been close.

Zone presses can speed up attacks, slow them down, or force them to make mistakes in ball handling. They can require opponents to concentrate more on their full-court offenses, taking time away from their half-court preparations. In most cases even when your competitors break your press, they will hurry their shots, helping your overall defensive game. Your press does not have to intercept passes to be successful.

The zone presses do not need selling. You know their worth. The question is not should you use them, but how, where, and when.

Zone press advocates usually choose between two plans: They teach one defense completely, i.e., the 2-2-1 zone press, developing different slides and stunts to give it variety; or they tutor multiple defenses, such as the 2-2-1 press after made baskets, the 1-2-1-1 press after successful free throws, and the 1-3-1 trap after unsuccessful scoring attempts. Both plans receive broad treatment throughout the book.

Coaches who believe in teaching one defense well will find in this book that each zone press not only has its basic slides presented, both in words and in diagrams, but alternate slides and maneuvers receive full illustration and explanation. Each zone press has another section concentrating on stunts that will give you many plural coverages from only one defense. What that one press intends to do, what it cannot accomplish, and the personnel needed to make it work will receive maximum attention. Adjustments to your opponents mode of attack will share a portion of the chapter devoted to your press. In fact, you can anticipate your opponent's adaptations. You will learn how to change the pace of your press— "off" or "on"; "fan" or "funnel"; "trapping"; "laning"; or "containing."

5

Those who believe in multiple defenses will find that they can choose any of the basic slides, alternate slides, stunts, or adjustments from each of the presses to make up their seasonal game plan. Chapter 10 gives you assorted ideas on how to formulate a multiple defensive system.

All popular full, half, and three-quarter court zone presses receive extensive individual exploration. Each zone press reveals proven techniques. Every avenue has been explored, researched, and clinically examined so that you can have at your fingertips the most thorough and complete analysis ever published on the zone presses. It is so complete that you can employ any of the zone presses for the entire game, changing its pace, intensity, and slides at your will, without allowing your opponent even one layup.

Even the lesser known presses have sections devoted to them. Chapter 4, for example, considers the match-up zone press, the 1-1-1-1-1 zone press, and the two plus triangle zone press among other hybrids. Chapter 8 covers the less popular half-court zone traps. Chapter 9 will show you how to recover from your favorite zone press into the half-court defense of your preference. Well-coordinated retreating and regrouping makes your press. Proper recovery allows you to run your press all night long and not succumb to a well-drilled, skillfully adjusting team.

Chapter 1 includes all individual and team fundamental zone pressing techniques. Without these basics, no press will succeed; with these foundations, even the weakest press will not only prevail but prosper. Each individual and team tactic also has a drill to help you tutor that mechanic until it becomes instinctive.

Refer to the section that *you* need to research. This will save you considerable time during those hectic, time-consuming winter months.

The drills and fundamentals along with the basic slides will make your favorite zone press solid and triumphant. Now add to this base the complete presentation of each zone press and a versatile multiple defensive system offered in *Basketball's Zone Presses: A Complete Coaching Guide*. This book will be a treasured reference work.

Burrall Paye

Contents

The Psychology of Zone Pressing 12

Seven Cardinal Principles of Zone Pressing 13

18 Individual and Team Techniques for Zone Pressing 20

1. "Off" and "On" • 2. Face-Guarding • 3. Denial • 4. Playing Man—Rotating to a Zone • 5. Drawing Charges Away from the Ball • 6. Short-Stopping • 7. Center-Fielding • 8. Left-Fielder • 9. Trapping • 10. Laning • 11. Containment • 12. Channeling • 13. The Peel-Back • 14. Give-the-Outside, Take-It-Away • 15. Run-and-Jump Stunts • 16. Defense of the Throwback Passes • 17. Stopping the Successful Attacking Pass • 18. Successful Retreating

Drills to Prepare the Individual and Team for Zone Pressure 36

One-on-One Control Drill • Double-Team Trapping Drill • Shooting the Gap for Steals Drill • Anticipation Drill • Double-Team, Anticipating, and Gap Shooting Combination Drill • Run-and-Jump Zone Press Drills • Two-on-Two Run-and-Jump Drill • Three-on-Three Run-and-Jump Drill • Three-on-Two Run-and-Jump Drill • Combination Run-and-Jump, Hedge, and Trapping Drill • Throwback Pass Drill • Recovery Drills • Safety Drills • Full-Court Horseshoe Drill

Summary 55

The 2-2-1 Zone Press: The Box Press 58

Personnel Needed for the 2-2-1 Press • Duties of Each Position • What the 2-2-1 Press Can Accomplish • What the

2-2-1 Press Will Not Do • Where and When to Use the 2-2-1
Press • Basic Slides of the 2-2-1 Press • Alternate Slides of
the 2-2-1 Press • Combining Slides to Reduce Offensive
Efficiency • Changing the Pace of the 2-2-1 Press

The 2-1-2 Zone Press 69

Personnel Needed for the 2-1-2 Zone Press • Duties of Each
Position • What the 2-1-2 Press Can Accomplish • What the
2-1-2 Press Cannot Do • Where and When to Use the 2-1-2
Press • Basic Slides of the 2-1-2 Zone Press • Alternate Slides
of the 2-1-2 Press • Combining Slides to Reduce Offensive
Efficiency • Changing the Pace of the 2-1-2 Press

The Diamond Press (1-2-1-1) and Its Variation (3-1-1) 81

Characteristics for Personnel of the Diamond Press • Duties
of Each Position • What the Diamond Press Can
Accomplish • What the Diamond Press Cannot Do • Where
and When to Use the 1-2-1-1 Full-Court Press • Basic Slides
of the Diamond Press • Alternate Slides of the Diamond
Press • Combining Slides to Reduce Offensive
Efficiency • Changing the Pace of the Diamond Press

The Jug Press (1-2-2) and Its Variation (3-2) 94

Personnel Needed for the Jug and Its Variation • Duties of
Each Position • What the Jug Press Can Accomplish • What
the Jug Press Will Not Do • Where and When to Use the Jug
Press • Basic Slides of the Jug Press • Alternating Slides of
the 1-2-2 and 3-2 Presses • Combining Slides to Reduce
Offensive Efficiency • Changing the Pace of Your Jug Press

The Match-Up 105

Start Man and Rotate to a Zone • Start Zone and Stay in a
Zone

The Minor Zone Presses 112

Y Press • The 2-1-1 Plus a Monster • The 1-1-1-1-1 • Two
Plus Triangle • Rebound Zone Press

Even Front Drop-Back Presses 125

The 2-2-1 Drop-Back Press • The 2-1-2 Drop-Back Press

1

Individual and Team Pressing Techniques

Zone presses are infinite in their variations, but always similar in their essentials. Many techniques are common to all zone presses regardless of their initial alignment. Their traps or stunts might occur at different spots on the court, but their objectives are the same. These fundamentals must be mastered to the point of being instinctive before your zone press can reach championship potential. Otherwise, any shortcomings will magnify themselves against your best-drilled, well-oiled opponent. Fundamentals are frequently overlooked by the inexperienced coach as well as by the experienced. Yet they are the basics for the development of your zone press.

Under no circumstances do you want to use all the tactics described in this chapter during any one year. Use only the ones that best exemplify the characteristics and skills of your current players. Save the others for those years which better fit the new personnel.

Drilling develops individual players which in turn stretches the force and the power of the team's zone press. Your zone press will never be better than the weakest defender executing it. But your zone press can improve immeasurably by training those weaker defenders. With the *right* personnel and with *proper* execution, where each defender assumes his role correctly, your zone press will counteract its own disadvantages.

THE PSYCHOLOGY OF ZONE PRESSING

Panic

Creating panic is the first and best reason given by most proponents of the zone press. Zone presses create chaos and fear in opponents more quickly than any other defensive tactic. Once an offensive team succumbs, it seems it can never fully recover. A good zone press club can come from far down to a comfortable victory in a matter of minutes.

Diversity

Each zone press is effective by itself, or when coupled with other zone presses to offer a plural or multiple look. Use any or all of the 18 techniques for zone pressing later in this chapter. Or you can switch from one zone, such as a 2-2-1 press used to slow down an opponent's attack, to another zone press, such as the 1-2-1-1, which is used to speed up the tempo of the game. All 18 techniques can be used with all zone presses. Once these techniques are learned, switching them from one basic zone press alignment to another becomes easy.

Structure

A zone press is skeletal in shape, making it easy to teach, simple to learn, and effortless for you to control. Unlike its man-to-man counterpart, which depends upon individual reaction to offensive maneuvers, the zone press is designed to compel an offense into spots desired by the defense. If this does not take place, you and your players know who did not perform their basic tasks, who is at fault, and what must be done to rectify it. This structural approach can also be considered a weakness. Too much structure can lead to a loss of initiative and, in the end, a weaker performance. You can use some of the basic 18 techniques in section three by allowing individual freedom or initiative. The more experienced your personnel, the more freedom you can allow. The less experienced should be held to the basics. In time, they'll become experienced; first they must do the common things uncommonly well.

Anguish

Your zone press will be broken physically many times, but it will continually cause mental pains even while physically failing. In fact, it causes anguish in your opponents' practice sessions whether you intend to employ it against them or not. Once you establish a reputation for pressing, your opponents will work against it in practice, often negatively, maybe even creating a fearful approach long before game time.

Unity

Team defensive unity is built because it forces a complete team defensive effort on every possession. This carries over to offense, to off-the-floor activities. Before long each member thinks of himself as part of a unit, not as an individual. Zone presses bring out the best in the meaning of the word team defense.

SEVEN CARDINAL PRINCIPLES OF ZONE PRESSING

Regardless of the zone press alignment or the objectives you intend to use, there are seven basic team tenets:

1. Defending Ahead of the Ball. By being ahead of the ball, all defenders can see the ball's location on the court and anticipate the ball handler's intentions. It is easier to react as a unit to those offensive moves when all defenders are above the line of the ball. Team members can put into operation a team strategy or stunt only if all team members are ahead of the ball. When the ball is passed or dribbled by the front line of the zone, the other defenders must hold up the attack until the front line can recover. By requiring all defenders to be ahead of the ball, you remove all loafing, you keep any defender from giving up on a play, and you impel all defenders to react completely as a unit. Most of the time, even when the press has been hopelessly broken, if all defenders initially began ahead of the ball, they can recover sufficiently to prevent an easy or uncontested shot. It is not the function of zone presses to steal every pass. But it is their purpose never to give an easy uncontested shot.

2. Double-Teaming and Trapping. In order to defend using a zone press, certain defenders are charged with the responsibility of forcing offensive action. These defenders must double-team, run-and-jump exchange, or trap the ball handlers, which will compel the offense to act. This defensive operation usually involves only two defenders, but the other three team members must know where and when this double-teaming and trapping will begin. These three off-the-ball defenders must act at the exact instant the trapping two commence their movement. Only when these five act *in unison* can you be sure your zone press is operating at its maximum efficiency. (Trapping techniques are explained later in this chapter.)

3. Gapping Attackers Away from the Ball. As two defenders trap the ball, the remaining three gap (zone the passing lanes) the other four attackers. They accomplish this by constantly floating away from the ball. As they see the trap closing on the ball, these gapping defenders keep their proper spacing (Diagram 1-1). Player 1 throws the ball into 2. X1 and X2 trap 2; 1 steps in to receive a return pass. X3 gaps 1 and the downcourt receiver 3. X3 will move a step toward 1 when 2 watches 1 or pivots toward 1. X3 will move a step toward 3 when 2 looks toward 3 or turns in that direction. X3 keeps his feet in motion, moving toward 2 if 2 does not choose to pass toward either 1 or 3. This movement forward increases X3's jump toward either the passing lane to 1 or the passing lane to 3. Any movement except backward will give X3 a quicker lateral (interception) motion. It is best for X3 to move toward the intended passing lane as 2 pivots to pass, but it is second best to move toward 2 if 2 does not quickly choose a passing lane. Also this will make X3 more aggressive, and it gives him a better angle to shoot the gap for the interception.

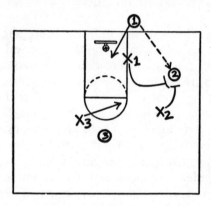

DIAGRAM 1-1

First, the three defenders away from the ball float to pick off any pass before the double-team. Then as the double-teamers begin their action, the floating three get into the gaps of the passing lanes, using the proper spacing techniques described previously. They keep their feet in motion so their movement to intercept will be quicker.

These gap shooters should watch the passer's eyes. All passers against double-team pressure look where they intend to throw the ball. If the passer eyes the vertical lane, the defender should fence-slide a step or two toward the vertical lane. If it appears to the passer that the vertical lane is covered, he will eye the diagonal lane. The gap shooter responds by fence-sliding toward the diagonal lane. This fence-slide serves two purposes: It delays the offensive passing attack, and it gets the defender in motion toward the area the ball handler watches, toward the intended pass, toward the interception. To be successful the fence-slide must be a positive aggressive slide. It must occur without crossing the feet, and the defender should remain on the balls of his feet. The defender must have no doubts.

Should the ball handler successfully complete his pass, the gap defender must arrive as the ball reaches the new receiver. He might draw the charge, force a walk, or flick the ball out of the grasp of a careless receiver. But he must at least require this new receiver to take a moment to consider his next action. This momentary pause gives the other four defenders time to reach their new location and assignments as the zone press continues into its second phase.

Defenders, while physically floating, must mentally play the passing lanes (Diagrams 1-2 and 1-3). Diagram 1-2 shows the passing lanes from a sideline ball position; Diagram 1-3 depicts the passing lanes from a middle court ball position. These passing lanes remain the same regardless of how deep downcourt the ball has penetrated. The passing lanes are always horizontal, vertical, and the bisector between them (the diagonals). The defenders away from the ball have the responsibility of gapping these passing lanes (playing directly between these lanes). When the ball is on the sideline, you need only two defenders to gap the three lanes. The other guard is a safety. When the ball is in the middle of the court, you need four defenders to gap the five lanes. This is mathematically impossible if you are trapping with two. Many coaches try to force the ball down the sidelines before trapping. Alert offensive coaches refuse to go down the sideline. An astute defensive coach abandons his

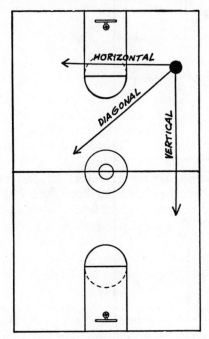

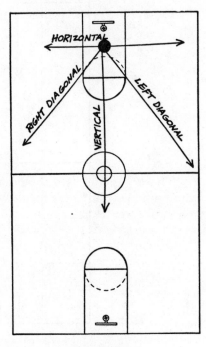

DIAGRAM 1-2   DIAGRAM 1-3

zone press or seeks a solution to gapping when the ball goes to the middle of the court.

Two possible zone solutions have emerged over the years. Play all attackers with the ball in the middle of the court with only one defender pressuring very hard. Gap with the other four where needed, possibly using only three gappers and employing a safety. When the ball leaves the middle of the court, trap with two, gap with two, and run a safety. The other possibility: double-team the ball in the middle and gap the vertical and the two bisector lanes (diagonals), leaving the other defender as a safety. This leaves open the horizontal passing lanes; both being nonpenetrating.

Another variation is to call off the zone press and go man-to-man whenever there is a successful pass into the middle area of the court. Although from time to time we will discuss switching from man-to-man to zone or from zone to man-to-man, this book is devoted primarily to zone coverages.

4. Forcing the Pass Where the Defense Wants It. Diagram 1-4 shows the best areas on the court for zone defenses to activate their traps. The favored region is represented by 1, and 2 shows the next preferred spot. Both of these primary locations are down the sidelines, but there

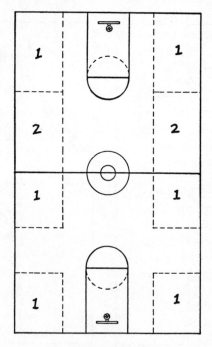

DIAGRAM 1-4

are certain zone press strategies that would encourage the traps down the middle lane.

Before any traps are set, just after the ball has been inbounded or even before the inbound pass, you may choose to deny passes to the middle lane, to the sidelines, or to both. Choices may change from game to game, from time-out to time-out, from team to team, or from quarter to quarter. Once a trap has been set, the defense might try to take away downcourt passing lanes, whether down the sidelines (vertical) or down the middle (diagonal), and give the horizontal passing lane.

Where the ball goes is not as important as having the defense direct it there. Plans must be made, drilled on, and carried out. Only in this manner does your defense dictate to the offense. If your defense cannot dictate to the offense, then you should change your defensive concepts. Sudden defeat awaits the defense which reacts to offensive dictates.

Dictation comes easier than domination. It is one thing to force the ball where the defense wants it; it is another to dominate play once the ball gets there. To impel the ball to a spot on the floor, merely leave the passing lane to that locale open while denying passes down the center lanes. During the hectic moments of an actual game, the ball usually follows the lines of least resistance. Have patience: sooner or later, even the best-drilled teams will take the ball down the avenues where they encounter no interference.

5. Forcing the Dribble Where the Defense Wants It. Although most teams attack zone presses with some type of team passing patterns, modern guards have advanced the dribble to an art form and many coaches are allowing these skilled dribblers to apply their specialty toward defeating opposing zone presses. Astute offensive coaches have plans which incorporate both the dribble and the pass.

A top-flight defensive team not only will compel the pass to a better defensive spot on the floor but will also impel the dribbler there. To accomplish this, the dribbler's defender should play in an overload of a half-step or more, depending on the relative quickness of the attacker and the defender, in the direction away from where the defense wants the offense to go. This defender should also maintain at least a three-foot horizontal cushion. This will prevent the dribbler from driving by the defender. It also means slower ball movement by the offense—a dribble will never cover the distance as quickly as a pass. This slower ball movement works to the zone press's advantage. Couple this soft play with retreating defenders in the path of the dribbler and the ball will move to the placement the defense wanted. The retreating defenders can suddenly spring the trap and snare the habit pass or the continuing dribble.

Should the attacker pick up his dribble to pass the ball before he dribbles to the preplanned defensive spot, the team defense must play to force the pass there. It does not matter how the ball gets to the locale—by pass or by dribble—it matters only that the ball is directed there by the defense.

6. Stopping Breakaway Dribbler with Weakside Deep Defender. On some nights your zone press will work miracles. On other nights you might have to jump into it, then out of it, into it, then out of it. Later you might jump back into it and it will work well. Even on the night when your press works extremely well, there will be possessions when it will be badly beaten.

Whenever the offense breaks your press you must have an organized and practiced retreat. This reassembling of your personnel not only can eliminate any easy basket by the breakaway attackers, but these retreating defenders can frequently slip into a passing lane for a quick steal.

Two avenues must be practiced: one for the defender stopping the ball and the other for the remaining four. The ball can advance by dribble or by pass. This section will stop the dribbler; the next section puts the brakes on the pass.

In all our defenses, man-to-man or zone, full-court or half-court, one rule remains constant: The deepest defender on the weakside must stop the breakaway dribbler (Diagram 1-5). This rule serves four pur-

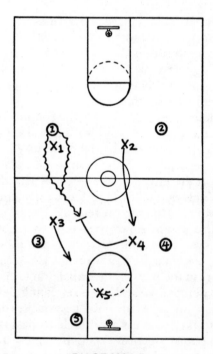

DIAGRAM 1-5

poses: (1) It commands the weakside always to see the ball, (2) it requires the other four defenders to retreat into the habitual passing lanes, (3) it frequently leaves a safety at home near the basket, and (4) it compels the attackers to make at least one more pass before they can score.

Diagram 1-5 exhibits all four of these advantages from this one basic rule. Player 1 drives by X1. It does not matter which side, left or right. X2 or X3 was out of position, allowing 1 to get by the first line of defense. They should have closed the gap. X4, the deepest weakside defender, came hard to stop 1. X4 wants to stop 1 as high on the floor as he can, turning 1 to the nearest outside line. To do this X4 must approach 1 hard but under control. His legs must be flexed and in motion. This enables him to move quickly in all directions. X4 wants to keep a cushion so that 1 cannot continue his drive. He overplays 1 one-half-a-man opposite the direction he wants 1 to drive. X4 should never relax his stance; too many players have advanced hesitation dribble maneuvers. Once X4 has cut 1 toward the sidelines, he must not let 1 turn the corner; he must force his movement back to the middle. There are fewer passing lanes from the sidelines. But once 1 starts back to the middle more passing lanes open; also there are many more defenders to deflect or intercept this pass as well as to help X4 on the continued drive. X4 begs 1 for recovery time.

Notice the four purposes have all been served. The weakside defender had to be alert to the ball, or he could not have picked up the dribbler, 1. X2 and X3 have retreated down the line of the dribbler, placing them in the two most prominent passing lanes. X5, the safety, has defended the area of the basket during the entire play. X1 cannot possibly make it through this defensive maze all the way to the basket. He must make at least one more pass, or he can shoot the ball off the dribble under tight duress. Shooting the ball quickly aids the zone press as much as a turnover would. No zone press intends to steal the ball on every possession. But if the zone press can force a quick shot, it means the opponents have probably taken a poor-percentage shot without proper floor balance.

Weakside deepest defender stops the breakaway dribbler. How do the other four retreat? The man beaten by the dribbler, X1 in diagram 1-5, races alongside the dribbler until he sees X4 pick him up. This prevents 1 from using both hands: X1 would steal or deflect a dribble on his side of 1's body. It also eliminates one escape route for 1. After X4 picks up the dribbler, X1 moves into the lane, never letting a cutter get between himself and the ball handler. X2 and X3 retreat quickly down the floor into the two immediate passing lanes, one on the left and one on the right. X5 guards the basket. If no pass comes immediately from 1, X1, X2, X3, and X5 all are inside the lane readying themselves for their half-court defense. When 1 passes back outside to begin the half-court attack, X4 joins his teammates in their called half-court defense.

7. Retreating While Pass Is in the Air. If proper spacing and preferred floating has occurred, the completed downcourt pass offers little chance of leading to a score. But an alert defensive team will have preparations made and practiced for all eventualities.

A defender in the passing lane, and there will always be one assigned, has two options. The press's success relies on this defender's judgment. This passing lane defender can gamble for the interception. If he gets it or deflects it, he used good judgment. If he misses, the new pass receiver becomes a breakaway dribbler and must be stopped, using the idea in section six. Let's use Diagram 1-5 as an example. Suppose 1 passed to 3, and X3 gambled but missed. X4, the weakside deep defender, should have floated as the pass went from 1 to 3. X4 now must stop 3, the breakaway dribbler, while the other defenders retreat in their ordered fashion.

This passing-lane defender's other option is to arrive as the ball arrives. Using Diagram 1-5 again: As 3 received the pass, X3 wants to be almost against 3, using aggressive hand and feet motion. Player 3 might walk or he might present the ball to X3, whereby X3's quick hand motion would deflect it out of 3's hands. If he began his drive too quickly 3 might charge. At the least, 3 would take a moment to review the new situation. This moment and the time the ball flew from 1 to 3 initially would allow the other four defenders to retreat to their half-court stations. A reception followed by a quick pass by 3 is frequently stolen by the retreating X1, X2, X4, or X5.

Defenders off the ball must react while the pass is in the air. A good drill to teach these defenders the advantage of retreating while the pass is in the air is to station a passer at midcourt, 1 in Diagram 1-6. Player 1 passes to 3 who quickly passes to the breaking 4 for the lay-in. Meanwhile, X2 has raced while the pass from 1 to 3 is in the air and while the pass from 3 to 4 is in the air. X2 will steal or deflect the second pass. After the defenders see they can cover a half-court length under two quick passes, they will have learned the great advantage to retreating while the pass is in the air.

18 INDIVIDUAL AND TEAM TECHNIQUES FOR ZONE PRESSING

All zone presses regardless of their initial and secondary alignments and assignments operate under the seven cardinal principles previously listed. All zone presses have common elements which occur and reoccur at different spots, locations, and times. These reoccurring elements are the individual and the team fundamentals of all zone presses. By spacing these tenets at different spots and times, zone presses give a plural appearance: They look different when, in reality, all have

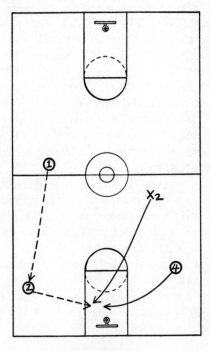

DIAGRAM 1-6

common threads. You'll notice all 18 of the following techniques can be incorporated into each of the zone presses presented in the latter parts of this book. Under no circumstances would you want all 18 in use during any one season. You, as coach, must decide which best suits your personality, your personnel's skills and personality, and which will best defeat the personalities of the clubs you'll face. All can be carried over from one year to the next, making each one taught accumulative in your program. You can begin teaching a particular zone press in the early years of your program. Then you can add different portions of the basic 18 as each year drifts by. This way your one zone press will have a plural look by the time it is used on the varsity level. In your hands rest these important decisions: one zone press with many of the basic 18; or several zone presses, each using only a few of the basic 18. Both ideas will give you more than adequate defensive firepower. Your other major decision is *when* do you start your teaching—eighth grade, freshmen, junior varsity?

1. "Off" and "On." You face three decisions nightly when you play the zone press: Where to apply the pressure? When to apply the pressure? How much pressure to apply? The simplest and maybe the most confusing part play of the zone press is the tactic of "off" and "on." You begin your season teaching the 2-2-1 zone press. You tell your players to race to this alignment after every score. "On" would mean that whatever basic technique you called, for example, the 2-2-1 peel back, would be activated as the ball is tossed inbounds. "Off" would mean the 2-2-1 would pressure the ball, giving the appearance of running the 2-2-1 peel back, but each player would drop and contain as the ball is advanced up the court. "Off" allows you to observe your opponent's mode of attack. It lures them into a false sense of security, yet it keeps the pressure on and tires your opponents physically and mentally. "On" activated after "off" intensifies the pressure.

"Off" and "on" gives your defense its first plural appearance. "Off" allows you to exaggerate your sluffs and floats, enabling your defenders to pick off lob or poorly thrown passes. "Off" encourages the opposition to advance the ball by dribble. Yet the opposition will get into trouble advancing the ball by a dribble when you activate "on." "Off" permits you to run the press the entire night, even when your opponents are beating "on." "Off" can strike fear and confusion in the minds of the opposition, for they never know when to suspect "on" and its many stunts. If you use "on" to force the opponents down the sidelines, and most zone presses do, you should use "off" to compel the ball to the middle.

To run "off," have the player covering the ball handler play him extremely tight, forcing him to dribble or pass immediately. Have the other four defenders drift at least two-thirds the distance from the ball to the receivers in their territory. You must at all times give the appearance of zone pressing. If this ball handler passes the ball, it should be under tremendous pressure from his defender; the pass, if the floaters have properly spaced themselves, should be intercepted. The ball handler will probably dribble, a maneuver he'll be wary of after he has faced "on" a few times. You have planted the seeds of doubt in the dribbler's mind. "On" will cultivate the rewards.

2. Face-Guarding. First you need a method to keep your opponents from inbounding the ball. Sometimes you will need to get a five-second call, or you will need to force a turnover. Face-guarding offers your squad this individual and team technique. It can be used from any full-court zone press alignment.

To face-guard the inbounds receivers, the defenders simply face their men. It is best to stay a few feet away from the receiver toward the passer, but the defender must not be so far away that he permits an easy inbound lob. Not too far away and yet not too close will always be relative: It depends on your defender's quickness and the quickness and faking ability of the receiver. This face-guard defender can pick up the intentions of the receiver by watching his eyes, studying his moves early in a contest, or a coach can help with a thorough scouting report.

The dual purpose of the face-guard is to impel the lob pass inbounds which might be picked off by a defender further downcourt or to force a bounce or chest pass which the face-guard defender can deflect or steal. Either way you create a turnover. Even if the inbounds pass is completed, the attacker still must negotiate 90 feet of floor space against four other downcourt defenders. Most of the time the dribbler's assigned man can regain a proper defensive position and still continue his harassment.

There are many ways your team defense can aid your face-guard defenders. You can put a defender on the out-of-bounds passer, trying to hinder his view as well as harass him. You must always have an assigned defender to help on the lob pass, otherwise you negate the purpose of the face-guard. You can accomplish these tactics from almost any zone press alignment.

3. Denial. Denial differs slightly from face-guard. While face-guarding, the defender sees only his man; while denying, the defender will see both his man and the ball. Frequently a defender who begins in a face-guard position will slip into denial when offensive movement occurs.

Denial defenders do not need a teammate further downcourt to intercept or deflect a lob pass. Denial defenders see the pass from its inception. They can bring their own man under control even if he successfully receives the inbounds pass. Denial defenders, by seeing both their man and the ball, can easily deflect any chest or bounce pass directed to their man if they can force their assignment to a receiving position 15 feet or more from the ball or if they can get their assignment to move away from the passer to receive the pass.

To play denial defense, the defender must have his head, a leg, and an arm in the lane between the ball and his assignment. The defender focuses his eyes at a point between the intended receiver and the ball: This allows him to see both the man and the ball. He should have a cushion of about three feet (depending on quickness differential of the receiver and the defender). He should prevent any movement toward the ball by beating his man to the pre-determined spot, forcing his assignment as far away from the passer as he will go. Being in motion, even before his man moves, will allow the defender quicker recoveries on any sudden and quick movement by his assignment. Grabbing at the floor with his toes or quick movement toward the receiver are proper examples of this pre-motion. On lob passes, the denial defender wants to put his body against his assignment's body and lean into the receiver as he tries to deflect the pass.

Team techniques can aid these denial defenders just as they do the face-guard defenders. Putting a defender on the out-of-bounds passer hampers his vision and encourages a hurried or unsure pass. Placing a teammate further downcourt with run and jump instructions on the intended receiver, or floating rules to intercept the lob passes, or trapping the inbounds receiver are all examples of team help to the denial defenders. All these tactics will receive examination during the latter sections of this chapter.

4. Playing Man—Rotating to a Zone. Many zone-press advocates use man-to-man face-guard or denial principles until the ball is received inbounds. Then the assigned defender and a teammate will trap this receiver. The other three defenders play the two downcourt passing lanes and a safety position further downcourt. To change from this man-to-man coverage to zone defense requires a set of rules that all defenders understand. Drills must make these coverages instinctive in each athlete. Nothing is left to chance. *No press is better than a poorly prepared one.*

Every zone-press alignment permits use of this team strategy. In later chapters we will describe some rules that will allow man-to-man coverage initially and evolve into the zone press of your choice.

5. Drawing Charges Away from the Ball. An offensive receiver racing upfloor but looking back downcourt at the passer offers an alert defender an opportunity to draw the charge. The defender must allow this attacker several steps in which to avoid the collision had the attacker known the defender would have already secured a position on the floor.

A patterned team which consistently breaks off a screen to receive the inbounds pass is a prime target for the defender wishing to draw the charge. This attacker must also be allowed a step or so. When breaking toward the ball, the receiver should see his defender. A defender on the player breaking to the ball must have both feet on the floor and already be in a stationary position prior to contact. An attacker who has been body-checked from a denial or a face-guard positioning frequently will continue a step or so. An alert defender accentuates the contact by falling to the floor. This defensive action, sometimes judged acting, should bring many favorable whistles from the official.

To draw the charge away from the ball requires some physical courage. The defender should take the contact in the torso, fall to the floor, roll on his back, and leave his upper legs at a 90-degree angle to his body. This prevents injury when the attacker falls on the defender. The defender should plan his movement so he is always stationary with both feet firmly planted on the floor at the moment of contact. Distance is required only if the player is looking back downcourt for a pass. Feet planted on the floor is required on all cutters, on all players without the ball. You do not need to give the player with the ball any distance, and your feet do not have to be planted on the floor. The player who is guarding the man with the ball takes the blow in the torso. It is the attacker's responsibility to get his head and shoulders in front of the defender before he drives.

6. Short-Stopping. When you employ a short-stop in your zone press, you double-team one inbounds receiver. Use this tactic when you want to keep the ball away from a particular attacker. Some teams have that exceptional dribbler-ball handler-passer. They design their offense against a zone press to get this man the ball and let him do his magic. By short-stopping, you can impel the ball toward a weaker ball handler-passer. If a team has become accustomed to the star ball handler receiving all inbounds passes, short-stopping this ball handler could disrupt your opponent's offense enough to bring victory.

How does one short-stop? You can have two defenders play in the lane between the ball and the star receiver. The defenders can play side by side or they can play one in front of the receiver and one behind. Playing side by side makes any lateral movement, left or right, have instant coverage. A vertical break after a right or left fake movement could get the star open. Side-by-side coverage also permits the lob pass.

When you have one exceptionally good face-guarder, it is best to place him in front of the star and put another defender behind the star. This coverage eliminates the lob pass, and it avoids the confusion of who covers the vertical cut to the ball after a fake right or left. Judging the skills and the favorite movements of the star could be the determining factor between parallel (side by side) or tandem defensive short-stopping.

Short-stopping can occur from either the even or the odd zone presses. When odd, you can assign the point and a wing to short-stop; when even, you can designate the two front defenders to short-stop. The ball will be inbounded down the line of least resistance to the nonstar ball handler. This may be just enough to provide victory.

Short-stopping can also be used to channel the ball to a desired defensive spot. A section on channeling follows later in this chapter.

7. Center-Fielding. When you face-guard or deny with your front-line defenders, you must have a specified defensive teammate located a short distance downcourt, probably between the free throw line and the midcourt line, to steal or deflect inbounded lob passes. This defender is called the center-fielder. He should be an alert, quick, basketball-wise individual. Size, although important, is secondary to speed and quickness.

Creative stunts can originate using the center-fielder. For example, the center-fielder can call for the denial defender to double-team or he can ask the denial defender to leave his man and become a second line defender while the ex-center-fielder covers the lob pass receiver. Many of these stunts will receive treatment in later chapters.

8. Left-Fielder. All zone presses have a left-fielder, a safety defender. This defensive man must possess size or its substitute, great jumping ability. He is the last line of defense, the 1 in the 2-2-1, for example. He must never allow a layup. He should never leave the basket position unless he sees that a teammate can cover the basket area: It is better to allow the jump shot than the layup.

Left-fielders begin their defense, if they possess any quickness, between the top of their defensive key and the time line. But as the ball advances downcourt, they retreat to the area of the basket. If you desire, they can become part of the rotation into the passing lanes and maybe even become involved in trapping. In future chapters, some zone presses involving left-fielders into the rotation and into trapping strategies will be presented.

Short-stopping, center-fielding, and left-fielding were terms originated for basketball by Morgan Wootten at DeMatha High School. He used them in man-to-man nomenclature. They have been expanded here to include the pressure zones. Their duties and positioning on the court, however, have not changed.

9. Trapping. Zone presses can be subdivided into three major categories: those that trap, those that lane, and those that contain. Trapping presses create chaos quicker than the other two types, but they are also the most vulnerable. Trapping presses can primarily spring their traps only at one position on the court, or they can have a secondary area, or they can devise even a third trapping zone. When offenses do not expect the trap, it operates at maximum effectiveness. Therefore, it is best to pluralize the dimensions of your zone press: one time show a laning zone press, next possession disclose the trapping press. In time your press will be the better for it.

Single trapping zone presses should recover without conceding even one layup. Regardless of the area the pass heads toward, one defender will have the responsibility of shooting the gap. The other four players should retreat while the pass is in the air. They should not stand and look to see if the pass is intercepted.

Double trapping zone presses grant more layups. Presses that plan three different trapping areas would allow even more. You must decide if safety or gambling is more the personality of you and your ball club. If you choose to double-trap, you should get more steals. You can plan triple traps and keep even more pressure on.

Trapping defenders should close on the ball in a manner from which there can be no escape. There should be a horizontal defender (container) and a vertical defender (trapper). The container should never allow a dribbler to drive to his outside horizontally or to drive outside by back pedaling before continuing down the floor. The trapper should never allow vertical penetration, and he should never permit outside penetration along the sidelines. Both the trapper and the container should close at a 90-degree angle. Both are responsible for preventing the drive between the two defenders, and the convergence at a 90-degree angle aids in preventing this splitting drive. The knees and the toes of the inside feet and legs of the two trapping defenders should touch while they are trapping.

Once the dribble stops, the two trappers should close tighter and pressure the potential passer aggressively with constant purposeful arm motion. This pressure should be designed to force a bad pass not to pick the ball out of the ball handler's hands. Picking the ball frequently results in a foul releasing the ball handler from a bad situation. The trappers should keep their hands in the same plane of the ball: If the ball is held high, the defender's hands are high; if the ball is lowered, the defender's hands are lowered. By keeping the hands in the same plane as the ball, defenders can deflect many passes. Even if the attackers manage to pass the ball without a deflection occurring, the passer would have to move the ball again before he passed it. This momentary pause might be enough delay to permit the trapper's teammates to intercept the pass, especially if they have properly spaced themselves and have anticipated the proper passing lane.

Most high school players get intimidated when trapped, and they will look directly at their targets. Teach your gap shooters to watch the eyes of the passer.

When a player catches the ball and the trap is immediately applied, the attacker still may dribble, so he must be covered differently. Tight 90-degree pressure would allow the passer-dribbler to step through the trap and dribble downcourt, so a loose trap must be applied. Both defenders, the trapper and the container, should be a few feet away, encouraging the dribble. They should keep their hands high, inviting the bounce or lob pass. Both of these passes could be stolen: the bounce and the lob are two of the slowest passes in basketball. Once the dribble begins, the two defenders close their trap as described above. Should this attacker pick up his dribble, the defenders close quickly, keeping their hands in the plane of the ball.

Should the dribbler break around the outside of the trap to freedom, a flicking move can be taught. The defender on the escape side steps completely around the dribbler. He is now behind the dribbler. He may even have to race upcourt to catch the escaped dribbler. He flicks the ball from behind. This type of flicking works only if the dribbler has beaten the trapper completely.

10. Laning. Some zone presses work better using laning techniques instead of trapping. Many zone presses can use both. Trading techniques with each changing possession can confuse well-drilled opponents.

When the defense lanes, it has only one defender on the ball. The ball can be stopped by two or more defenders using some stunt or strategy that will cause the dribbler to kill his dribble. Trapping before laning, for example, forces the dribbler to stop dribbling. If the container were to rotate into a passing lane prior to a pass from the trapped dribbler, then laning would be in effect. The peel back, giving the outside before taking it away, the run and jumps are all excellent stunts that can use either trapping or laning tactics.

While laning the defense will have only one defender on the ball and the dribble will have been killed. At least three and maybe all four of the other defenders will locate between the ball and the potential receivers. This puts these defenders in the passing lanes, forcing a lob pass for further penetration. These lob passes are easy prey for the interception. "Used" tells defenders the dribble has been killed and for the gap shooters to hurry to their assignments. When five seconds elapse without a pass, the defense gets the ball.

11. Containment. Any zone press alignment is easily used for containment. Containment means the defenders will allow the ball to be slowly marched downcourt, usually by dribbling. One defender covers the ball handler while the others play just out of the passing lanes. A soft pass or one thrown to the defender's side of the attacker might be stolen. Otherwise the ball can be advanced by passing. At all times the ball can be dribbled into frontcourt. The defender on the dribbler might force zigzag movement.

Containment is a decoy strategy. A team allowed to advance the ball by dribbling, for example, will face some defensive maneuver in later possessions that will kill the dribble. Usually these stunts occur just as the offense gets complacent because of the containment strategy.

Hedging goes hand in hand with containment. A nearby defender helps the defender guarding the ball by faking toward the ball handler and then retreating. This nearby defender can, in any one possession, activate the tactic of hedging several times. If the dribbler picks up the ball, the defender off the ball can slide into the passing lanes, activating laning maneuvers. If the dribbler moves up floor by hesitating and then advancing at every hedging maneuver he sees, then the defensive strategy of containment is working. "Off," which can be used in conjunction with all zone presses, illustrates perfect containment.

12. Channeling. Successful defenses direct the ball, by pass or by dribble, to a favored location on the floor. When all team members know the direction the ball is to be sent, they can all react more quickly to called defensive stunts or maneuvers. When they know further where this direction will occur, full-court, three-quarter court, time-line, half-court, etc., their presses will work at maximum efficiency. So two defensive strategems are involved: where on the court does the defense apply the pressure, and in which direction does the defense intend to compel the offense.

You can channel in the beginning by denying one side the ball and not pressuring the passing lanes to the other side. You can put a defender on the out-of-bounds passer, exaggerating this defender to the denial side of the court. Or you can shortstop one side and leave the other side open. Or you can play the open side with a loose defensive strategy. The ball will enter the court on the nondenial side because there is little or no resistance.

Once the ball is on the court, you decide to fan or funnel. *Fan* means the defense will force the ball down the sidelines, and *funnel* will impel the attack down the middle. By overplaying the ball handler yet keeping a proper cushion, the dribbler can be encouraged to drive in a desired direction. The overplay is about half-a-man opposite the direction you want the dribble to go. The proper cushion prevents the dribbler from driving past his defender. This cushion varies with the speed and quickness of the two players involved. Each must determine his own safe distance: The closer the defender can play the dribbler the more pressure he can apply and the more mistakes he can force. But the dribbler must never be played so closely that he dribbles by his defender.

Which side of the court do you want to force the dribbler toward? By forcing the ball up the offensive left side, you impel right-handed players to use their weak hands. By forcing the ball up the defensive left sideline when trapping, you gain the advantage of being away from the trail official. A small foul might not be heard or called. Another advantage of forcing the ball down one distinct sideline on every possession: All players become specialists. The container and the trapper are always the same defenders. The two gap shooters are always the same. So is the safety. This tactic will enable you to place your best trappers in the area of the trap, your best gap shooters where they will always be shooting the gaps.

Teammates of the defender on the ball help to determine the direction of the pass. By denying a pass in one direction but playing the passing lane soft in another, offenses usually, when under game duress, attack the softly defended passing lane, the line of least resistance.

Numbers or letters can designate areas of defensive attack. Forty or *A* could be full-court. Thirty or *B* could represent three-quarter court. Twenty or *C* could mean a half-court press. A 1-2-1-1 forty face-guard fan press would tell us: Deny the ball inbounds, force the attack outside once the ball is inbounded while using a 1-2-1-1 alignment. A trap or a stunt would occur on the sidelines just after the ball has been received inbounds. The ball would be channeled to the sideline, trapped or stunted; and the defense would have the advantage of knowing in advance when and where it would occur, making it easier for the defense to act in concert, to act as one, to cheat in the direction of the planned trap.

13. The-Peel-Back. Stunts, such as the peel-back, should be taught in pairs. A stunt that gives away the middle should be followed by one that is strong in the middle. The peel-back and the give-the-outside-then-take-it-away are two stunts that cover for one another. Where the peel-back is weak, give-outside-and-take-it-away is strong and vice versa. They complement each other.

Diagram 1-7 displays the peel-back tactic. The defense begins in a 2-2-1 alignment, fanning to the outside, expecting to set the trap in the three-quarter court (thirty) area. The call: 2-2-1 fan thirty peel-back. X1 forces the dribbler down the side line. X4 drops in his lane to discourage the lobpass. X4 can hedge, jump toward 1 and then move back, if it appears X1 might lose 1. X2 denies 2 any pass horizontally or diagonally downcourt. X3 floats and X5 plays safety.

After 1 begins his dribble downcourt, and the outside lane does appear open, X2 begins to drift to 1's side of the court. If 1 picks up his dribble to pass to 2 (a very difficult task if X1 has properly located himself in that lane), X2 must race back to cover 2. If 1 continues dribbling downcourt and X1 has offered enough pressure, then X2 races ahead of the ball, gets into the outside passing lane, and *peels back* down the lane to set the trap with X1. X3 knows when this is to occur (thirty), and he prepares himself to cover the habit passing lane across court to 2 as well as the diagonal lane toward 3. X4 covers the vertical passing lane (to 4) and the diagonal lane (to 3). X5 anticipates any lob, and he plays safety.

Peel-backs work well with all zone presses, but they work best after "off" has been run a few possessions. "Off" encourages your opponents to dribble the ball upcourt. The opponent becomes complacent, thinking it easy to drive outside or inside at will. He "sees" the outside lane open, begins his drive, fully confident it will be open, but he is met by a peel-back maneuver. Frequently, this type possession ends in a turnover.

14. Give-the-Outside, Take-It-Away. This stunt complements the peel-back, and it can also be used in all zone press alignments. It works best after the offense has become accustomed to dribbling downcourt.

Diagram 1-8 exhibits the 2-2-1 zone press fan thirty give-the-outside-then-take-it-away defensive call. Diagram 1-8 is exactly the same call as Diagram 1-7 except the stunt was changed from the peel-back to give-the-outside-then-take-it-away. X1 encourages 1 to drive down the sideline (fan). X1 pressures 1 to prevent 1 from spotting any open receivers. X4 drops in the outside lane, creating the illusion to 1 that the lane is indeed open. X4 can hedge to slow 1 down if he feels 1 is breaking free from X1. Under no circumstance should X4 allow the lob pass to 4. X2 denies any horizontal or diagonal downcourt pass to 2. X3 floats off 3, protecting the middle. X5 plays safety but checks any lob pass to 3 or to 4. This coverage by X1's teammates encourages 1 to dribble. An "off"

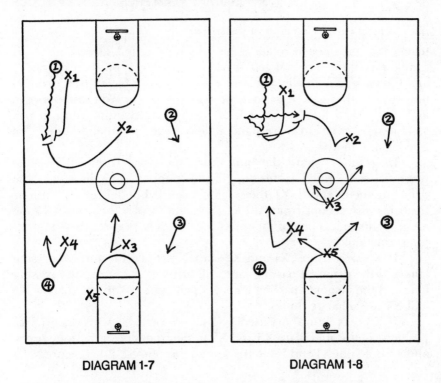

DIAGRAM 1-7   DIAGRAM 1-8

or any containment strategy immediately preceding give-the-outside-take-it-away makes the stunt that much more effective.

After 1 begins to dribble a few steps, X1 cuts off further penetration down the sideline. Then 1 must change direction, charge, or pick up his dribble. If 1 picks up his dribble, the passing lanes are covered and X1 closes in quickly putting his hands in the same plane of the ball. As 1 reverses or crossover-dribbles, X2 springs toward him, arriving just as 1 completes his move. A change could result. X1 and X2 trap. X3 moves to cover the horizontal passing lane to 2 and the diagonal passing lane to 3. X4 repositions himself to cover the vertical passing lane to 4 and the diagonal passing lane to 3. X5 plays safety, preparing for any lob pass he may pick off or any breakaway threats to the basket.

15. Run-and-Jump Stunts. Although run-and-jump stunts began exclusively in the arena of man-to-man defense, they have recently been expanded to include the zone presses. These stunts will add yet another dimension to your favorite zone press.

You can run-and-jump "trap," or you can run-and-jump "jump." "Trap" tells the container to stay and to trap with the trapper, and "jump" requires the container to trade assignments with the trapper. Both stunts can become natural reactions between two players, or the bench can call them. Should the dribbler kill his dribble, the trapper can call "used," telling the container to rotate as he would in "jump." These three calls can be mixed or interchanged at will, depending upon the experience and the basketball intellect of your club. They can be left to individual initiative, or they can be as structured as you prefer. You can even run and "jump" and then follow it with another called stunt. You can run your regular zone press trap and follow it with a run-and-jump. The options are limitless.

Diagram 1-9 shows the "jump" and the "trap" from a 2-2-1 zone press. X1 has fanned 1 outside. X3, the trapper, runs directly at the dribbling shoulder of 1. X1, the container, keeps 1 under control until he hears his instructions from X3. X2, X4, and X5 play their normal zone assignments unless one of them has your consent to enter the run-and-jump rotation.

If X3 calls "trap," X1 and X3 trap. X4 covers the vertical passing lane and the diagonal passing lane; X2 blankets the horizontal passing lane and the diagonal passing lane. X5 plays safety. You could allow X5 and X4 to exchange duties.

If X3 calls "jump" or "used," X1 would rotate back to X3's original position. This would place X3 and X2 in the front line of the zone press, and it would put X1 and X4 in the second line of the 2-2-1 zone press. X1

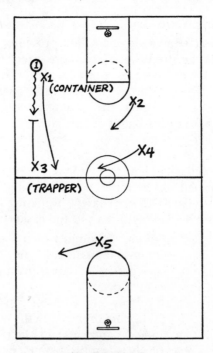

DIAGRAM 1-9

and X3 merely exchanged duties. They must know both area responsibilities. Because the 2-2-1 structure was never broken, the press can
continue. Another stunt can be activated, or the ball can be forced to
another trapping area. A third defender can join the rotation; for
example, say X4 rotates to the left passing lane and X1 rotates completely
around to X4's former position. You could allow all four to rotate; this
would put X3 on the ball, X4 where X3 started, X2 where X4 began, and
X1 filling in at X2's spot. The fewer players involved in the rotation the
less likely a mistake will occur.

Predetermine the skills and intellect of your players, and then your
rotation rule. Once made, you must stick by it, constantly drilling to
make it work. Your rule should cover every situation. A rule covering
one situation and another rule covering another situation would harm
the defense more than it would confuse the offense. Defense must be
more instinctive, and the more rules you make the less the defense
remains instinctive. A rule can be made instinctive by drilling, drilling,
drilling.

16. Defense of the Throwback Passes. Diagram 1-10 shows a
throwback pass. A throwback pass occurs when a pass is made crosscourt
out of a trap. This throwback pass can be short, or it can be long. Unless
you design your zone press for only single trapping situations, you must
have some guidelines to help your team cover throwback passes. These
rules should be simple, they should be uniform for all the zone presses
and stunts you intend to use, and they should have drills accompanying
them so the coverage will become instinctive.

In Diagram 1-10, the pass from 1 to 2 presents a short throwback
pass. A short throwback pass is a horizontal or a slightly forward pass
completed in front of the first gap shooter (X1 in Diagram 1-10). The
coverage rule for the short throwback pass would be something like this:
X1 contains 2 while X3, the original trapper responsible for the
horizontal driving lane, comes over to help X1 trap 2. X4 rotates the
length of the time line, gapping the new vertical pass (to 3) and the new
diagonal pass (to 4). X2 sags to the middle, defending the new horizontal
passing lane (to 1) and the new diagonal passing lane (to 4). X2 also
readies himself for the next throwback pass. Should the throwback pass
come back to 1, for example, X2 must contain 1 while X3 recovers again
to help X2 trap 1.

A pass from 1 to 3, the deep diagonal pass, is the long throwback
(Diagram 1-10). The long throwback, when successful, usually defeats
the frontal attack of the zone press. Its coverage rule would be different:
X4 races crosscourt at an angle that prevents 3 from driving inside to the
basket. X5 plays safety in case 3 gets away from X4. If, however, X5 is
mobile enough to become an interceptor, a gap shooter, you may want to
rule X5 as the stopper of the long throwback pass—the deep diagonal

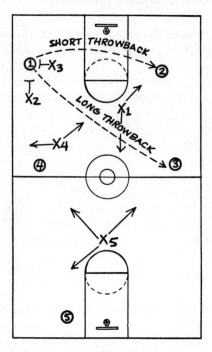

DIAGRAM 1-10

pass to 3. In this case X4 would rotate to safety and assume the basket-protecting duties. Or you could rule a second trap situation by having X1 trap with X4 and by having X2 and X3 rotate to the new vertical and horizontal passing lanes. Or you could rule that on all long throwback passes X2 and X3 would race to their new half-court defensive assignments while X4 (or X5) stops the dribbler (3). The rule you choose must be simple, must be the same for all your presses and stunts, and above all must correspond with your pressing philosophy.

A pass from 1 to 4 is not a throwback pass (Diagram 1-10). It would represent a vertical pass, a pass down the strong sidelines. Any zone press that does not call for only the single trap would have rules to trap 4's reception of this vertical pass (a second trapping situation).

Many zone press teams, unless they are extremely well drilled, give up after a completed throwback or vertical pass and they retreat to their half-court defense. By ruling your throwback coverages, the players will not get confused and you can develop a more aggressive zone press that has secondary and third trapping situations.

17. Stopping the Successful Attacking Pass. This is not a natural defensive movement. It must receive drilling and then reinforced drilling. After that, you still must *insist* on this defensive technique. Players will not naturally react to the vertical pass.

On any successful pass out of a trap, the defender who was assigned the area of the reception must arrive as the ball arrives. He must be prepared to contain and delay, contain and delay the next offensive move. As the pass touches the receiver's hands, the defender should be as close to the receiver as possible without the receiver escaping containment by dribbling. He should be prepared to retreat a step or two quickly. By requiring this aggressive maneuver, many defenders will not give up on the interception. Should they arrive late, they still might draw a charge if the attacker decides to drive immediately. The new pass-receiver might feel the defensive pressure and walk with the ball. He might pass hurriedly toward a teammate as he receives the ball. This quick pass leads to many interceptions or thrown away balls. The new receiver, if he has poise and experience, usually delays his next move until he has surveyed the situation. This, too, helps the defense. It gives the defenders time to reset their new assignments. Should the new receiver decide to put the ball on the floor and begin a dribble, his defender pushes him outside, and contains and delays. This new on-the-ball defender should have his knees flexed, his feet in motion, and his eyes on the plane where the ball is being held. As the attacker brings the ball down toward the dribbling position, this defender retreats a few steps (giving himself a cushion) and begins an overplay designed to force the drive outside. This outside route is always the longest to the basket, and it also eliminates a passing lane once the attacker gets nearer to the basket.

18. Successful Retreating. Proper defensive recovery makes your zone press. Not only will proper recovery reduce layups, but proper recovery is an extension of the press. It is the last chance to steal or deflect a pass. Teams that recover properly can press aggressively without fear of being beaten at the basket.

Rules must dictate how the weak side (the side away from the ball) will rotate. This rotation must cover the basket area and provide passing lane coverage there. It must also delay the attack long enough for the entire team to retreat to their half-court defense.

Diagram 1-11 illustrates a team recovery pattern. Player 1 passes to 2 who passes to 3. The deep weakside defender X3 recovers to the basket area as X5 goes out to cover 3. A pass from 3 to 4 would be intercepted by X3. Should 4 cut to the ball, X3 must remain between 4 and 3. X1, X2, and X4 must race inside the key before recovering to their half-court defensive positions. The weakside recovery rule is simple: Weakside deep defender covers basket area. The safety, X5, must not leave the basket area until he sees that the weakside deep defender, X3, can recover. X3 must beware of any cutter who tries to get between himself and the ball. X3 must force a lob pass or no pass. Frequently, the passer, 3, who has two defenders (X5 and X3) between himself and a teammate, cannot find a receiver.

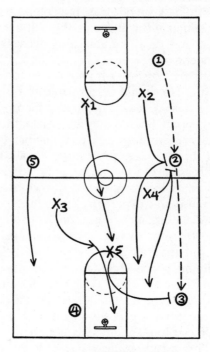

DIAGRAM 1-11

DRILLS TO PREPARE THE INDIVIDUAL
AND TEAM FOR ZONE PRESSURE

It does no good to prepare a team press unless its individual performers have been well grounded in the fundamentals of pressing. Once those individuals have mastered their art, then team drills will make the defensive tactics and slides instinctive. First the players, then the team concepts.

One-on-One Control Drill. Some coaches call this the zigzag defensive drill. It is used to teach the defensive players to steal, flick, and draw charges against the crossover dribble, the reverse or spin dribble, and the behind-the-back dribble. With inexperienced players you should begin by walking through the drill offensively and defensively. Teach and drill one defensive maneuver before moving on to the next. For example, teach your defender how to stop the crossover dribble. Later, teach that defender how to draw a charge against the crossover. Then advance to the reverse dribble and the defense of it.

Procedure (Diagram 1-12):

1. Put an offensive player and a defender in each line.

2. Limit the attacker to the reverse dribble, for example.

3. Begin by limiting the defender to flicking, to stealing, or to drawing the charge. Don't let the defender do all three.

4. After you feel the defender can flick, steal, and draw the charge, insist on the defense deciding which technique to use.

5. After attempting a flick, charge, or steal (successful or not), the ball, the attacker, and the defender return to the spot of the steal, flick, or charge and continue downfloor.

6. Three successful flicks, steals, or charges should occur in one full-court trip.

7. Attacker reverses downfloor and back before exchanging places with the defender.

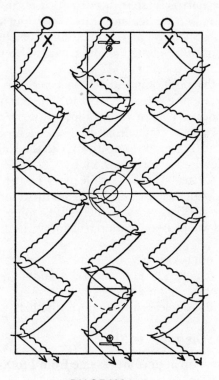

DIAGRAM 1-12

Objectives:

1. To teach flicking, stealing, and drawing the charge off the reverse.

2. To teach overplaying and recovering for another overplay.

3. To teach proper individual man-to-man pressure defense.

4. To teach the offensive reverse-dribble.

Double-Team Trapping Drill. There are two ways that double-teamers can steal the ball: steal the pass when thrown out of the trap, or tie up or steal the ball while it is still in the trap. An offensive player holding the ball while in frontcourt for five seconds commits a turnover. Stealing the pass is better since trying to steal the ball while held frequently leads to fouling, a foul that permits the offense to escape from a difficult situation. To force the bad pass, defenders should first permit the attacker to dribble—then apply the double-team. This eliminates one of the offensive moves. After he has started dribbling, you want the trapper to approach him with caution, never allowing him to split with a dribble. Once the offensive man has lost his dribble, assume a tight, narrow base. The narrow base is important; it encourages the bounce pass. Inside feet are perpendicular to each other. Outside arms are high, and inside arms are located at the knee and the shoulder. Arms are waved in a constant windmilling motion, trying to keep the hands in the same plane as the ball is being held.

Because of the positioning of the feet and the inside arms, it is almost impossible for the offensive man to step through an open area. He will make a bounce pass or throw a lob.

The offensive man could leave his feet. If he does, so does the defender. The attacker cannot come down with the ball without walking. Try to deflect a level pass, forcing the lob.

If you try to steal the ball while it is in the trap (this is not encouraged), you want to slap at the ball from the floor up. You want the defender to move his body toward the ball, keeping his hand on it by sheer hustle. This will give you a jump ball and you will try to recover the ensuing tip.

If the defender can get both hands on the ball, he should immediately begin a steady pull and then suddenly jerk down. The moment the defensive man feels his opponent giving, the defender should use his body as a lever to try to pry the ball loose.

Procedure (Diagram 1-13):

1. Line players up in one line. Rotate from 1 to X1 to X2 to the end of the line.

2. Coach passes to 1 to activate the drill.

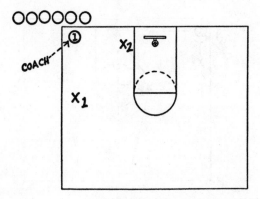

DIAGRAM 1-13

3. Player 1 tries to break the double-team by dribbling.

4. X1 tries to contain 1 until X2 arrives for the double-team.

5. Player 1 keeps the dribble alive while X1 and X2 force him into the corner. We like 1 to keep dribbling because it causes X1 and X2 to force him into the corner. This eliminates reaching in and fouling and trying to steal the dribble when double-teaming, a cardinal defensive sin.

Objectives:

1. To teach the dribbler to avoid the double-team.

2. To teach how to double-team correctly.

3. To teach one defender how to contain and another how to apply the trap. X1 prevents vertical advancement; X2 eliminates horizontal movement. They both prevent the split.

Shooting the Gap for Steals Drill. When playing a zone press you can have your players specialize. For example, you can force the ball down the right side of the court only. Two defenders there can always be your double-teamers. The left side is always your gap shooters. You can put your better anticipators there. It is best if you develop your entire team into a crew of double-teamers and gap shooters.

Procedure (Diagram 1-14):

1. Line players up in one line. Rotate from 1 to X1 to X2 to 3 to X3 to end of the line.

2. Coach passes to 1 to activate the drill.

3. Player 1 does not have a dribble, or the drill at this stage can be run like the double-teaming drill (Diagram 1-13) with X1 and X2 stopping the dribble.

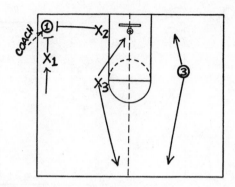

DIAGRAM 1-14

4. X1 and X2 double-team 1.

5. X3 stays within interception distance of 3, but not up against him.

6. Player 3 can move up and down the court but does not come across a half-court imaginary line (dotted).

7. After the double-team, 1 tries to pass to 3 and X3 tries to intercept. Player 1 must not lob pass.

Objectives:

1. To teach defenders how to shoot-the-gap and intercept passes.

2. To teach 1 how to pass under double-team pressure.

3. To teach double-teams the proper methods of forcing a bad pass in order to help X3 pick it off.

4. To teach X3 the perfect position from which to shoot the gap for the steal.

Anticipation Drill. Many players, when they begin organized basketball playing, do not understand the value of anticipating where the passer will throw the ball. This drill teaches those individuals how to read the passing motions of the man with the ball.

Procedure (Diagram 1-15):

1. Line players up as shown. Rotate from 1 to X1 to 2 to end of line.

2. A coach or the manager with the ball stands under the goal with his back to the three players. The passer pivots to his left as though he intends to pass to 1. X1 reads this and responds by getting in motion toward 1. The coach pivots back to his right. X1 reads this and gets in motion toward 2. X1 always keeps eye

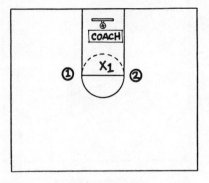

DIAGRAM 1-15

contact with the passer's eyes, and he watches the passer's passing motion. By keeping eye contact, he can usually tell where the passer will throw the ball. Most high school passers will pass where they are looking when under double-team pressure. By watching his arm motion, the defender will respond quicker to the actual moment the passer releases the ball.

Objectives:

1. To teach the defender to anticipate the moment of release.
2. To get the defender in motion toward the intended target.
3. To teach the defender the proper positioning so he can have an angle to intercept the pass without fouling. X1 should be a step or so in front of both 1 and 2. During this drill neither 1 nor 2 is allowed to move further than three feet outside the lane to receive the pass.

Double-Team, Anticipating, and Gap Shooting Combination Drill.

Procedure (Diagram 1-16):

1. Keep all defensive players on defense until they have played all four positions. Rotate from X1 to X2 to X3 to X4 after two possessions. Then rotate offensive and defensive units.
2. Pass the ball to 1. X1 and X2 begin to close in on the double-team. Player 1 can escape by dribble or pass.
3. X3 gaps 2 and 3. X4 gaps 3 and 4. Players 2, 3, and 4 cannot move to receive the ball.
4. X3 and X4 watch the eyes and passing motion of 1; 1 can throw any pass.

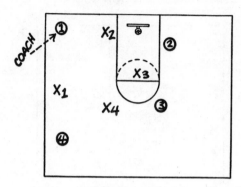

DIAGRAM 1-16

Objectives:

1. To teach X1 and X2 how to double-team trap a dribbler, and how to keep hands in same plane as the ball on the passer.
2. To teach 1 to pass out of the double-team, and how to dribble around the double-team.
3. To teach X3 and X4 proper positioning for shooting the gap.
4. To teach X3 and X4 how to anticipate the pass from 1.

Run-and-Jump Zone Press Drills. Before you teach your favorite zone press slides, you should study ways to incorporate run-and-jump stunts within the framework of your press. The following three drills are stunts. They can teach up to a three-man rotation in your run-and-jump zone press slides. The two-on-two stunt is developed by the two guards pressing the two men bringing the ball up the court (Diagram 1-17). It can also teach the guard and the forward to cooperate in a two-on-two stunt. The defender away from the dribbler races over to cover the vacated attacker. The three-on-three drill (Diagram 1-18) involves the same original move but in a different rotation: As the defender away from the dribbling guard races toward the dribbler, the defensive forward moves up to cover the open offensive guard and the dribbler's original defender rotates to the vacated attacking forward. The three-on-two stunt (Diagram 1-19) is used to stop two exceptionally talented ball handlers from advancing the ball. By using these stunts, any bad pass can be intercepted and any completed pass can still be covered by the slides of your zone press.

Two-on-Two Run-and-Jump Drill.

Procedure (Diagram 1-17):

1. Line players up in two lines. The offense advances the ball downcourt and back; then rotate from offense to defense to the end of the line.

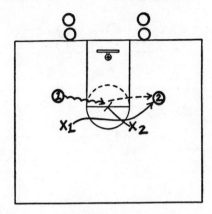

DIAGRAM 1-17

2. Player 1 dribbles but X1 will not let him outside. Player 2 may never get above him. X2 may never get below the line of the advancement of the ball.

3. When X2 wants, he runs directly at 1 as X1 forces inside. If 1 continues his dribble, he must charge X2 or veer outside. If he veers outside, X1 continues his pressure and X2 helps. If 1 picks up the ball to pass to 2, X2 tries to deflect it as X1 races to cover 2; continue this run-and-jump the length of the court and back. If X1 and X2 steal the ball, they fast-break. X1 and X2 hold their double-team as long as 1 continues his dribble. If 1 and 2 cross, X1 and X2 switch, creating the impression of a zone press.

Objectives:

1. To teach the defenders how to play run-and-jump defense.

2. To condition the athlete for pressure zone defense and fast-break offense.

3. To improve ball handling.

Three-on-three Run-and-Jump Drill.

Procedure (Diagram 1-18):

1. Line players up in three lines. The offense advances the ball downcourt and back; then rotate from offense to defense to the end of the line.

2. If 2, the center player, is dribbling, he must be going toward either 1 or 3. In either case, that is a two-on-two run-and-jump (see Diagram 1-17). However, if either 1 or 3 is dribbling, force him to the inside and run the three-on-three run-and-jump.

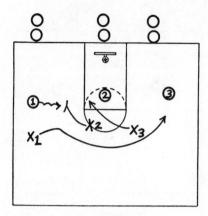

DIAGRAM 1-18

3. For the sake of discussion, let's have 1 drive to the inside and run the three-man run-and-jump. As 1 drives inside, X2 races toward 1 and double-teams with X1 until 1 puts both hands on the ball. This is X1's cue to race hard to cover 3. Meanwhile, X3 has shot the gap between 1 and 2 for the interception. Even if the pass is completed, you are still in a man-to-man coverage and can rotate the weakside man into the zone slides. If the offense should turn the ball over the defense can fast break. You should require that the two offensive men without the ball stay behind the advancement of the ball. That not only expedites teaching, but it permits more run-and-jumps per possession.

Objectives:

1. To teach three defensive men how to coordinate their efforts in a three-man run-and-jump.
2. To improve offensive ball handling.
3. To teach proper methods of double-teaming.
4. To teach shooting the gap.
5. To condition defensive players for full-court zone pressure, including rotating into the slides of your zone press.

Three-on-Two Run-and-Jump Drill.

Procedure (Diagram 1-19):

1. Line players up in two lines. The offense advances the ball downcourt and back. X3 starts at safety on the way downcourt and X1 starts at safety on the way back. X2 is the first safety when the two lines rotate after a trip downfloor and back.

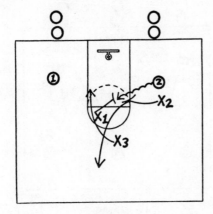

DIAGRAM 1-19

2. X1 and X2 run and jump switch or trap while X3 shoots the gap. After X1 and X2 stop 2's dribble, X2 drops and becomes the new short safety, waiting to shoot the gap on the next run-and-jump.

Objectives:

1. To teach three defenders how to run-and-jump against two attackers.
2. To condition defensively for full-court zone pressure.
3. To teach double-teaming and shooting the gap.
4. To improve the ball handlers offensively.

Combination Run-and-Jump, Hedge, and Trapping Drill. Because run-and-jump, hedging, and trapping are integral parts of zone pressure defense, you can expedite teaching by using this combination drill.

Procedure (Diagram 1-20):

1. Line players up in three lines. After each player has been through the drill, rotate the lines clockwise.
2. The first line learns to run-and-jump between the forward and guard spots. The second line learns to hedge yet recover in the passing lane for an interception. The third line learns runs and traps.

Objectives:

1. To teach X1 one-on-one control of the dribbler.
2. To teach X2 how to run-and-jump at the outside shoulder of the

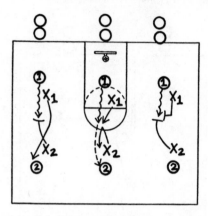

DIAGRAM 1-20

dribbler, how to hedge and recover in time to intercept a lob pass, and how to help X1 trap a dribbler.

Throwback Pass Drill. Some coaches trap the first pass (inbounds pass) and zone the passing lanes. They hope to steal the pass out of this trap. When this pass is successful, the defensive team retreats to their half-court defense. This is the weakest of the zone presses, and it is the safest, most conservative. It is known as a single-trapping zone press. It is more a stunt than a press.

If you advocate the above stunt as your complete press, you have no need for throwback pass drills. Most coaches, however, want more than one opportunity to trap and to steal passes out of those traps. Those coaches must have throwback pass coverages and drills to augment those assignments.

Throwback pass coverages can be as simple as one-on-one containment (as in most 2-2-1 zone presses); or a defender can contain the receiver while a defensive teammate comes hard to help trap this new receiver (as in most 1-2-1-1 zone presses). One-on-one containment is the same as in the zigzag drill (Diagram 1-12). Diagrams 1-21 and 1-22 are continuations of Diagram 1-16. A rule will be established for short throwback passes and for long throwback passes. You may have to create a throwback pass rule and formulate a drill that will correspond to that rule if your favorite zone press is considerably different from the ones presented in this book.

Procedure (Diagrams 1-21 and 1-22):

1. Line up four attackers at four corners of backcourt, using the 28-foot markers and the baseline as the bases of the rectangle.

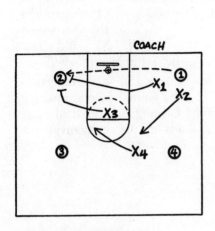

DIAGRAM 1-21

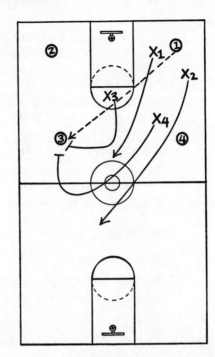

DIAGRAM 1-22

2. Put four defenders in a diamond formation as shown.

3. The coach stands out-of-bounds and passes into either 2 or 1 (1 in Diagram 1-21).

4. Player 1 tries to escape X1 and X2's trap as he did in Diagram 1-13.

5. Once 1's dribble has been stopped, X3 and X4 gap 2, 3, and 4. A pass from 1 to 2 (short), or a pass from 1 to 3 (long) would represent a throwback pass.

6. Player 1 passes to 2 in Diagram 1-21, a short throwback because it occurs in front of X3. X3 contains 2 while X1 comes to trap with X3. While the pass is in the air, X4 gaps 3 and 4, shading toward 3, and X2 gaps 1 and 4, shading toward 4.

7. A pass from 1 to 3 (Diagram 1-22) illustrates a long throwback because it occurs behind X3, the front-gap shooter. X4 arrives to 3 as 3 receives the ball. This frees X3 to try for the interception. If X3 cannot intercept, X4 must contain 3 until X3 can help trap. X1 and X2 rotate to their new positions while the pass is in the air.

8. A pass from 1 to 4 is not a throwback. It is a vertical attacking pass. But this pass can also be ruled and drilled on if you wish. A pass from 1 to 4 (see Diagram 1-22) would have X4 containing 4 and X2 helping X4 trap. X3 would rotate to the downcourt vertical passing lane (as X2 did in Diagram 1-22). X1 would rotate to the new diagonal passing lane as he did in Diagram 1-22.

9. Passes can continue back and forth, back and forth, especially between 1 and 2 until all defenders know their throwback coverage assignments instinctively. Drilling on this drill daily during the early preseason practice sessions pays great dividends during the later season.

Objectives:

1. To teach trapping.
2. To teach proper spacing and gapping.
3. To teach shooting the gaps for steals.
4. To teach throwback coverage rules.
5. To teach all the basic assignments of your zone press.

Recovery Drills. Not all passes are going to be stolen. Many will be completed. Your press will be broken more times than you will intercept or deflect. Even when your press has been physically broken, it will have taken its mental toll. The secret to successful pressing is not allowing the offense an advantage even though they may physically break the press. This mandates a recovery drill.

Procedure (Diagrams 1-23 and 1-24):

1. Line up five offensive players and two defenders as shown in Diagram 1-23.
2. Player 1 passes to 2 who passes to 3 who passes to 4. All of these passes are rapid, thrown as they are received.
3. X3 begins to race downfloor as 1 passes to 2.
4. When 4 receives the ball, X5 goes out to cover him. Player 5 breaks to the basket for a pass from 4. X3 must get to the basket before 5 gets there. X3 should be able to deflect or steal any pass from 4 to 5.
5. Alternate passing route: When 2 receives the ball he can bypass 3 and pass directly to either 4 or 5. When 3 receives the pass he can pass to 5 as well as 4. This keeps X5 honest. It also allows X5 to practice being a long pass interceptor. If 5 receives a pass, 4 breaks to the basket. X3 must prevent pass to 4 for the layup should 5 receive a pass from 3 or 2.

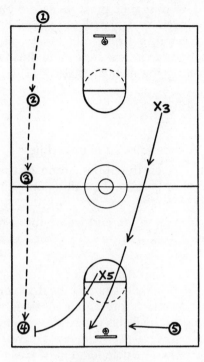

DIAGRAM 1-23

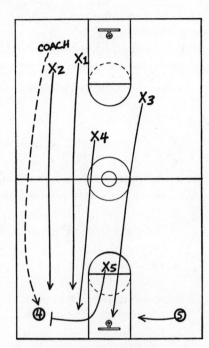

DIAGRAM 1-24

6. Players 4 and 5 can play two-on-two against X3 and X5. Player 3 can break to head of the circle and make the drill a three-on-two after the safety drills have been learned.

7. Diagram 1-24 depicts a full-court team recovery drill. You can make a baseball pass to either 4 or 5. All team members must arrive to half-court defensive stations before 4 can pass to 5.

Objectives:

1. To teach that proper recovery never allows a layup. The defenders quickly see that they are never too late if they hustle.

2. To teach X5 to intercept long passes.

3. To teach X5 to stay home until he sees that X3 can recover to the basket area.

4. To teach two-on-two and three-on-two safety coverages.

5. To teach defensive movement while pass is in the air.

Safety Drills. You have drilled on individual control, double-team trapping, shooting the gap for steals, throwbacks (so you can teach a second and a third chance to trap), and a recovery drill for a last ditch effort to steal a pass. You have drilled on your zone press slides and on the stunts you intend to use. Now you need a safety drill so you can be assured your opponent will not score even if they physically break your press. We will offer three safety drills. You can interchange them during the season to help keep your team from going mentally stale.

(A.) Three-on-two-on-one

Procedure:

1. Place your entire team in three even lines on one baseline.

2. Place two defenders at the basket on the opposite end of the court. They should play tandem or parallel, depending on your defensive safety philosophy.

3. The three attackers dribble or pass to the end where the two defenders are. They end their attack in a three-line fast-break form.

4. One defender stops the ball. The other defender takes the first pass receiver. The defender who originally stopped the dribbler drops to the basket area on the first pass, preventing a pass to a player under the basket. Whenever the ball is passed the second time, the defender under the basket rotates to the new receiver, trying to get there as the ball arrives. The defender on the passer races to cover the area near the basket. They continue this rotation until they steal a pass, give up a score, or rebound a missed shot. The defenders will be successful if they can force two passes before a shot results; in a game situation their three teammates would have had sufficient time to recover.

5. If the original dribbler had continued his drive to the basket, his original defender would stop him by trying to draw the charge or he would stay with the dribbler while his teammate would zone the area under the basket.

6. Whenever a shot is taken, the two defenders attack to the opposite basket. The man taking the shot retreats in a two-on-one defensive situation. Should a pass be deflected or stolen, the two defenders attack the opposite basket. The player responsible for the turnover becomes the defensive player in a two-on-one situation.

7. The two members of the original attacking three remain on defense for the next three-on-two situation. Regardless of what happens in the two-on-one, the next three players in the line attack the two at the far end of the court and the drill continues.

8. The top defender of the two should pick his man up as high as possible out on the court to force an early decision.

Objectives:

1. To teach safety defense: Three-on-two and two-on-one.

2. To teach attacking by three lanes against two, and to teach two attackers how to attack one defender. Because your defenders are outnumbered, you might want to teach an attacking defensive stunt. You could have your front line defender cut the dribbler left. The back line defender could race up the lane at the dribbler, station himself, and try to draw the charge. Most dribblers pass but do not stop. The front defender, when he hears "jump," could rotate to the basket area with hands up, hoping to deflect a pass. Instead of the back defender racing up the lane, he could show himself in the left passing lane, and at the exact moment the dribbler intended to pass to his right, the deep defender could rotate to his left. If he gets there in time, he steals the pass he had anticipated. If he gets there late, he prepares to draw the charge. Many team safety techniques can be taught that will give the advantage back to the defense.

(B.) Three-on-three call

Procedure:

1. Place the entire team in three lines on the baseline. These players are attackers.

2. Take the front three out to the free throw line, have them face the three lines on the baseline, each member at the free throw line paired with an attacker on the baseline. The three men at the free throw line are defenders.

3. Stand at the free throw line tossing the ball to one of your players on the baseline. The defender paired with that attacker must touch the baseline before racing to the other end of the court to help on the three-on-two situation.

4. The three-on-two situation occurs because the three attackers fast-break to the opposite end of the court while the remaining two defenders try to stop the attackers.

5. Go to the other end and place the same three on defense and run the drill back. The original attackers become defenders when they have attacked down the floor and back.

Objectives:

1. To teach retreating to a two-defender tandem. One must take the ball and let his teammate know he has the ball. He yells "ball." His teammate retreats to the area of the basket.

2. To teach the third defender that by hustling he frequently can get back to help the two defenders and make it a three-on-three situation.

3. To teach safety defense: Three-on-two.

4. To teach a three-lane fast-break attack.

(C.) Three-on-Three-on-Three-on-Three

Procedure (Diagram 1-25):

1. Line 12 players up as shown. If you keep more players, place them in lines behind 4, 5, and 6 (Diagram 1-25).

2. This is a continuous three-on-three-and three-on-three drill. Run it for about 12 minutes or to a score of ten for maximum conditioning.

3. Player 2 has a ball and 1, 2, and 3 attack A and B. C cannot help stop the attack. C receives the outlet pass if 1, 2, or 3 misses the shot, or C receives the inbounds pass should 1, 2, and 3 score.

4. After A, B, and C begin their break downfloor, 1, 2, and 3 stay on defense: two in tandem, the other as an outlet pass receiver.

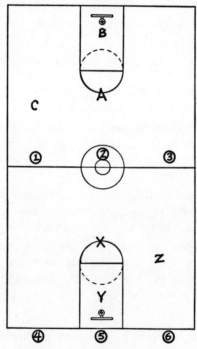

DIAGRAM 1-25

5. A, B, and C attack X and Y. Z, like C, cannot help.

6. When X, Y, and Z begin their attack on 1, 2, and 3; 4, 5, and 6 step onto the court. A, B, and C step off the court onto the baseline. In a moment 1, 2, and 3 will get the ball from X, Y, and Z. Players 1, 2, and 3 will immediately attack 4, 5, and 6. The drill continues.

7. After three-on-three-on-three has been run several days, you can allow the attackers to score then turn defenders and man-to-man or three-man zone press. For example, 1, 2, and 3 score. Now A, B, and C must bring the ball inbounds. Players 1, 2, and 3 can press A, B, and C to midcourt. The ball, in this case, must be dribbled across midcourt or X could pick off any long pass. This brings a press into the three-on-three-on-three drill. The press continues every time one of the groups score. Quickly defenders realize they can score several baskets in succession when they press as a unit.

8. You can run the drill as a four-on-four-on-four by allowing each team another outlet pass receiver. This really brings the press into play, and it includes the four lane number break if you're a teacher of such a method of play.

Objectives:

1. To teach safety defense: Three-on-two.

2. To teach outlet pass and the three-lane fast break.

3. To condition your team to press.

4. To teach confidence in press breaking.

5. To teach alertness—must constantly be ready to defend and to attack.

6. To teach going from a score to your press positions.

7. To teach offense to go to their anti-press attack positions.

Full-Court Horseshoe Drill. After all the players have mastered the techniques of trapping, shooting the gaps, and the other team stunts and slides, a horseshoe drill that can be expanded or contracted at your discretion offers opportunities to drill on all team tactics or only on those methods not mastered.

Procedure (Diagram 1-26):

1. Line up four offensive players in each of the four corners in backcourt. Place one player out-of-bounds. He inbounds the ball.

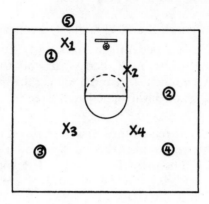

DIAGRAM 1-26

2. Line up your four backcourt defenders in the alignment of your full-court press. In Diagram 1-26 your zone press is the 2-2-1 face-guard. If you run a 1-2-1-1 zone press, you adjust the drill by placing the offense into a 1-2-1 shell set and put X1 on the out-of bounds passer. You could allow X3 to face-guard 1 and X4 to gap 3 and 4. This allows harassment of the inbounds pass.

3. You can work on any one of the following, mix up two or three, or work on all of them:

   a. Get ball inbounds against face-guard or denial: X1 and X2 face-guard or deny while X3 and X4 play centerfield.
   b. Let X1 and X2 shortstop 1, forcing ball to 2, then pressing.
   c. Allow X1 and X3 to exchange places on a lobbed inbounds pass (X2 and X4 if ball is thrown into 2). As the ball flies toward 1, X3 comes hard, arriving to 1 as the ball arrives. X1 rotates to second line of the defense.
   d. Run any stunt once the ball is inbounded: run and jump, give outside then take it away, peel back, basic traps of your zone press, etc.
   e. Permit only passing, including passing back out-of-bounds. This forces defenders to run their slides as the ball floats through the air.
   f. Make many throwback and vertical passes, requiring the defenders to know your throwback rules (short and long).
   g. Allow 1 or 2 to dribble drive, forcing the weakside deep defender to stop the breakaway dribbler.

Objectives:

1. To learn all the team tactics, slides, and rules of your favorite zone press.
2. To learn floor positioning, proper floats, and proper spacing.
3. To learn to recognize the passing lanes.
4. To get down the proper team rotations on all slides, stunts, etc.

SUMMARY

Zone presses must have methods of denying inbound passes: Faceguard and denial are two such tactics. They must have strategies to steal the lobbed pass inbounds: Leftfield and centerfield offer these opportunities. They must have tactics to force the attackers to do what the defense wants. Shortstopping and playing man before rotating to a zone are just two such maneuvers. They must have means to force a turnover before the ball is passed inbounds: drawing charges away from the ball grants this. Each zone press must have the three mechanisms to make itself plural: trapping, laning, and containment.

Once the ball has been inbounded, the zone press must have strategies that will confuse the attackers. "Off" and "On," channeling, the peel-back, give the outside then take it away, the run and jumps can easily confuse, especially when alternated from possession to possession. Once the attack conquers the defense, the defense must have a secondary plan; for example, coverage on throwback passes and stopping any successfully completed pass. Of course, when the secondary plan folds or succumbs to the attack, a method of recovering and preventing a shot must be planned, worked on during practice, and drilled, drilled, drilled so it will be instinctive.

This chapter explained zone pressure techniques in detail. This keeps repetition to a minimum while we explain the slides, stunts, and adjustments in chapters 2 through 8.

All stunts that work in man-to-man coverage also work in zone coverage. In man-to-man defense, these maneuvers are performed instinctively; in zone presses, these techniques are more structured. Most coaches prefer the structured.

There is no way every possible slide of every press can receive treatment in the following chapters. The options are infinite. Enough slides will receive exploration where a thinking coach might devise yet another. After settling on a press or several presses that best fit your personnel's skills, the important thing is to drill, drill, and drill on the slides until they are instinctive. Unless you can recruit players, you must depend on the skills in your program. Find the press that fits those skills or you must develop them.

2

Even Front
Full-Court Zone Presses

The most popular zone press in basketball, the 2-2-1 zone press, is also the safest. It has become known as the box press. The other even front zone press is the 2-1-2.

Press structures, slides, and adjustments are designed according to the defensive personnel, the opponent's personnel, the game situation, and the press's objectives. You cannot expect a zone press to accomplish something it was not made for.

Very few teams are surprised by a zone press anymore. All teams practice and work daily against expected presses, especially the box (2-2-1) and the diamond (1-2-1-1). How your opponents will react to your press, their personnel, and your evaluation of your personnel will determine to a large degree which of the explored adjustments and slides you intend to use. Your decisions will add a victory or subtract a loss because every team on your schedule can be beaten.

All these aspects of the 2-2-1 and the 2-1-2 receive extensive treatment in this chapter: the personnel needed to meet the objectives of your press, what the press can accomplish and what it cannot, the basic slides of the press, adjustments and stunts, combining those slides, and even changing the pace of the press.

THE 2-2-1 ZONE PRESS:
THE BOX PRESS

Personnel Needed for the 2-2-1 Press. Where you place your defenders and what type of skills they will need depends entirely on the objectives of your press. Diagram 2-1 shows the standard positioning of the 2-2-1 press. Each paragraph that follows explains who should be where depending on your press's objectives. For example, if you intend to deny you would want your quicker players up front; if you intend to steal lob passes you would want your quick interceptors in the second line.

If you intend to deny or face-guard the inbounds pass, X1 and X2 must be your two quickest players, probably the guards (Diagram 2-1). These defenders must encourage over-the-head passes. They will try to draw charges on players cutting to the ball. They automatically switch on picks or crisscross moves. Should the attacker they are denying or face-guarding break downcourt, they must go to the midcourt area before opening to see where the ball is. They must read their man's hands and eyes. They will always count to three (1,001, 1,002, etc.), and then they open to find the ball. Five seconds is a turnover, and that includes the time for the flight of the pass. The pass usually requires a second or two to complete.

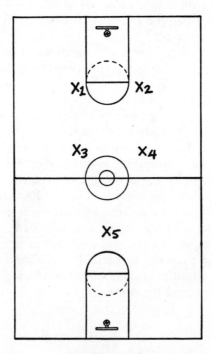

DIAGRAM 2-1

Most officials love to make the five-second call. If the pass comes into their man, they will trap, rotate, or contain, depending on the objectives of the press. If the pass goes away from them, they must hurriedly get into their assigned zone passing lanes. X1 must be the better defender of the two because many high school teams are right-handed. X3 also must be the better defender between himself and X4. These two would be your next two quickest defenders, probably your forwards. X3 would become your first monster man. He must be intelligent and quick; otherwise you should abandon plans to face-guard or deny. X3 anticipates where the ball is to enter the court by watching the motion of the man throwing the ball inbounds. Most attackers assigned to throw the ball inbounds look where they intend to throw it. X3 must pick up and deny the third attacker who comes downfloor. He must completely deny the third man the ball. X3 can change assignments with X1 or X2 on lob passes into X3's area. X3 can gamble for interceptions. When he gambles for interceptions, he can require X1 to jump as they exchange responsibilities. X3 and X1 can trap. X4 becomes the second monster man, picking up the fourth attacker coming downcourt. X4 has the same duties as X3. X3 and X4 play centerfield. X5 can be your slowest defender. He watches for long lob passes as he plays leftfield. He must never leave the area of the basket unless another teammate can cover the basket area for him.

If your wish is to run only the basic slides of the 2-2-1 press, you have three primary safe alignments. X1 and X2 can be guards, X3 and X4 forwards, and X5 center. This gives you more pressure on the ball, but it leaves you with less quick gap shooters. It also makes your defense vulnerable to quick passes downfloor before X5 can offensively rebound and get to his defensive position. If you prefer to allow the ball inbounds and push it outside before trapping, the two forwards at X1 and X2 might pay the best dividends. This strategy requires the attackers to pass over a taller defender to get the ball back to the middle. Your two guards could occupy X3 and X4, giving your quicker defenders the position of gap shooters and the difficult position of stopping dribbling penetration while trapping. X5 still plays center, and he can be the slowest defender.

The third best alignment when you consider only basic slides would put your quickest guard at X1, your second quickest forward at X2, your quickest forward at X3, and your center at X4. Your second quickest defender, who also is your second quickest guard, would occupy X5. This would mean you intended to put X5 into the rotation. This last alignment also is best against teams that throw long inbound passes. A lot of teams try to get the ball inbounds quickly after a score, and many of these teams throw the ball to midcourt or beyond. X5 would be the guard responsible for defensive balance. He would be in perfect position to play safety on the press and to steal any quickly thrown long pass.

Should you decide to run "stunts" and adjustments, you must decide which stunt or adjustment before you consider placement of personnel. If you intend to trap the throw-in and cover throw-back passes, X3 and X4 should be the guards. X1 and X2 are the forwards. If you intend run and jumps or peel-backs or give-outside-then-take-it-away, X1 and X2 must be your quickest, probably the guards. You could use the last alignment in the preceding paragraph for the stunts and adjustments. This alignment places your quickest players on the offensive right side of the court and your slower defenders on the left.

Duties of Each Position. Duties will be explained as we explore each diagram, each option. Duties change as the objectives of the stunt, slide, or adjustment vary.

What the 2-2-1 Press Can Accomplish. The 2-2-1 press is popular because of its versatility. You can contract (play defenders very close together, protecting the middle) to force the ball up the sidelines by pass or by dribble. You can expand (spread defenders from the middle out) to gamble for lob pass interceptions and to force flash pivots into the middle. You can push the ball to the corners near midcourt, then trap and play the passing lanes. You can trap immediately as the ball is inbounded; or you can deny the throw-in, hoping for a violation or an interception. You can run one of the many stunts discussed in chapter 1 to try to gain possession with a turnover. You can run "off," which offers constant harassment and will make "on" stunts more effective.

What the 2-2-1 Press Will Not Do. The press will not speed up play. Because of the safety features of this press, most teams attack it slowly, usually setting up their half-court offense each possession. This press can keep mental pressure on most of the game. It can cause late-game offensive fatigue. This press allows the opponents to make mistakes. The 2-2-1 does not frequently steal pass after pass after pass against good ball clubs. This press rarely, unless you run stunts, forces mistakes. It is more a patient press than one that will cause panic. But this press rarely if ever gives up easy layups or uncontested jump shots.

Where and When to Use the 2-2-1 Press. It is safe to use the 2-2-1 the entire game without worrying about the attackers adjusting and routing it. Because it is the safest zone press, teams adjusting to it still cannot overwhelm it. You cannot run the 2-2-1 when you are behind late in a game unless you intend to use quick, trapping-style stunts. It is not a ball-hawking, steal-producing press. It takes its toll over a long duration.

Where would you employ it? All over the court. You can deny inbounds passes, use stunts after the ball is inbounded, guide the ball to a particular spot, or utilize the basic slides and traps. Your designs solely determine where you will activate the 2-2-1's many options.

Basic Slides of the 2-2-1 Press. Diagrams 2-2 and 2-3 illustrate the basic slides of the 2-2-1 zone press. The abilities of X5 determine which basic slide you should use. If X5 is agile, quick, and able to read passing lanes, you should include him in the rotations (Diagram 2-2). If X5 is tall

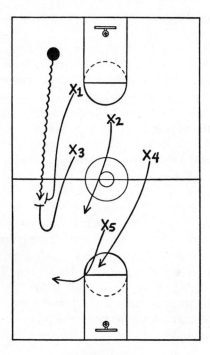

DIAGRAM 2-2

and a little slow but a good protector of the basket, use the slides of Diagram 2-3. You could teach both and use them alternately. Diagram 2-2 leaves the long lane near the basket open momentarily, but Diagram 2-3 closes that lane from inception. Diagram 2-2 offers maximum coverage on the vertical passing lane, and Diagram 2-3 sometimes shows that lane open.

In both cases X1 pressures the man with the ball at all times. X1 tries to keep the ball handler from spotting any open receiver while he is dribbling. X2 sags to the middle, cutting off that passing lane. If 1 wishes to pass horizontally to 2, X1 and X2 exchange duties. The press then provides an open lane down the opposite side of the floor. X1, in both diagrams, impels the dribbler down the sideline. The ballside deep defender, X3 in the diagrams, retreats, allowing the dribbler to "see" an open sideline. X3 prevents any lob pass to an attacker in the vertical passing lane. When 1, the dribbler, sees the apparent opening up the sidelines, an essential of trapping from the 2-2-1 has been fulfilled. X3 then sprints back to close the trap near the centerline. It is best to set this trap just as the dribbler crosses the timeline, but anywhere near the midcourt line is acceptable. While the offside up-defender, X2 in the diagram, drops to cover the middle, he also is responsible for the diagonal passing lane and the throwback pass. X4, the weakside deep defender, must guard against a flash pivot into the middle lane. He gets help from X2.

The slides differ when the trap is set. If you use X5 in the rotation, he takes the vertical passing lane (Diagram 2-2). X4 rotates quickly to cover the dangerous diagonal passing lane, the lane from the ball to the basket. X5 helps on the diagonal lane. X2 also helps on the short diagonal passing lane; the more help the safer the press. X2 mentally covers the horizontal passing lane. If X5 is not in the rotation, you have a safer press (Diagram 2-3). X4 then rotates over to the vertical passing lane. X2 still covers the short diagonal passing lane, and he anticipates a throwback horizontal pass.

Floaters X2, X4, and X5 must hover just outside their passing lanes. They must dash into the lane quickly once the ball is in the air. If they cannot intercept, they must reach the receiver as the ball arrives. This delays the receiver's next movement, giving the defense time to recover. These downcourt passing lane defenders cannot stand straight up and down in defensing attackers in their area. They must be in a helping stance so they can see most of the court.

Pursuit and retreat angles of the two trappers, X1 and X3, are paramount. X3, for example, must receive drilling and drilling so he will know the exact moment to sprint to set the trap. He must move before

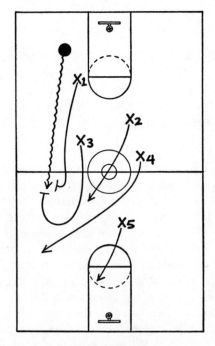

DIAGRAM 2-3

the dribbler can cut inside, but if he moves too soon the dribbler can brush past him on the sidelines. X1 must always have a cushion so that 1 cannot drive by him to the middle. In setting this trap X3 should place his foot within six inches of the sideline because skillful ball handlers need less than a foot to drive. X3 must be able to sprint quickly, and he must be able to stop equally as quick. He should have his hands high as he comes to meet the driver. This encourages the lob or bounce pass, the two easiest passes to steal. Both X1 and X3 must approach the trap from the inside of the court out.

X5, the safety, must not come out to stop a jumper in a two-on-one situation (X4 in Diagram 2-2). Stopping the layup is the safety's job. Once a shot is taken, the safety must prepare himself for the rebound. Other defenders must quickly retreat (see proper recovery in chapters 1 and 9).

The twin dangers in pressing are always present: (1) Failure to fall back quickly enough when the press is broken; or (2) giving up on the press when it still has a chance to work. These seem contradictory; only you can decide where one ends and the other begins.

Alternate Slides of the 2-2-1 Press. You can add many alternate slides to your basic slide. You can make your press as complicated or as simple as you wish. In no way should you incorporate all during any one season. A single press becomes multiple whenever it has many planned options.

(A.) Traps in the middle passing lane. The primary objective of the 2-2-1 zone press is to keep the ball out of the center lane. It sometimes reaches there by pass and by dribble. If it does, you may prefer to admit your press is broken and fall back to your half-court defense, or you may wish to continue and trap again.

Diagram 2-4 exhibits a drive by 1 into the middle lane. X2 comes to trap. Instead of trapping, you could let X2 drop into the middle and let X1 force 1 down the left offensive sideline. Or you could let X2 cut off 1's penetration and let X1 drop to the middle. If 1 picks up his dribble, X1, X3, and X4 could cover three passing lanes; the press could continue on any successful horizontal or backward pass. If X1 and X2 trap, X3 and X4 must read their passing lane coverage. X3 and X4, when in doubt, would want to cover receivers from the inside of the court out. X5 would read his coverage, protecting the basket area first. Most successful passes out of this trap must still face the recovering 2-2-1 press.

Diagram 2-5 displays an invert. Player 1 passes the ball successfully into the middle lane to 3. X4 was responsible for denial to the flash pivot, but a breakdown allowed 3 the ball. Player 1 could have advanced the ball to the middle lane spot by dribbling past X1 and X2 (weakside deep defender must stop breakaway dribbler, as told in chapter 1). Under either condition, X4 must arrive as the ball arrives. X4 might draw the charge, force a walk, steal a loosely held ball. But X4 must, under all

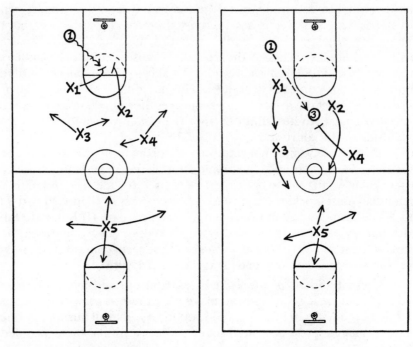

DIAGRAM 2-4   DIAGRAM 2-5

conditions, delay 3 a second or two. While the pass is in the air and while X4 delays 3, X2 inverts and exchanges positions and responsibilities with X4. X3 drops to cover weakside middle. X1 drops above the advancement of the ball. X5 plays safety. When teams attack the center lane, they like to slip a pass to a cutter down the weakside sideline. X2 could deflect this pass. If X5 is alert and anticipates, especially after a successful pass or two, X5 can pick off this pass. Such coverage is not dangerous because X3 can retreat to the basket area. Under invert, X1 and X4 play up front, X3 and X2 defend the secondary line, and X5 plays safety. And the 2-2-1 press is still on.

(B.) *Run-and-Jump.* In Diagram 2-6, when the dribbler goes down the sideline (fan), X3 must run at the dribbling hand of 1. X1 hears "jump" and exchanges places with X3. X5 can enter the rotation telling X1 to play safety. Under no circumstances should four defenders rotate; you should limit it to two or three, depending on X5's skills. The weak side drops to normal floater coverage.

Diagram 2-7 illustrates the run-and-jump when the dribbler funnels. X2 stops 1's advancement. X1 rotates when X2 commands "jump." X4 can enter the rotation, compelling X1 to rotate to X4's old position. X3 drops to the middle, and X5 shades in the direction of the dribbler.

X3 could call "trap" in Diagram 2-6. This activates the basic slides of either Diagrams 2-2 or 2-3 (your choice). X2 could call "trap" in Diagram

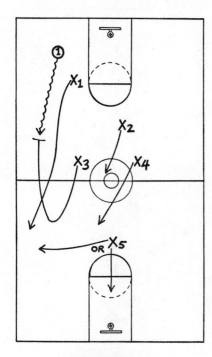

DIAGRAM 2-6

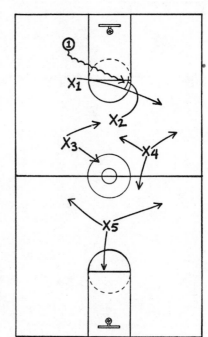

DIAGRAM 2-7

2-7. This impels the coverage of Diagram 2-4. You, as coach, can "jump" but not "trap," "trap" but not "jump," or do both. On any of the jumps, if the dribbler picks up the ball, you have the three downcourt lanes covered plus a safety. When the dribbler does pick up the ball, his defender (X2 in Diagram 2-7 and X3 in Diagram 2-6) must blanket him, yelling, with constant arm and leg movement. A hurriedly thrown pass will be intercepted. A successful pass still must face the 2-2-1 press with added duress because most of the ten seconds have vanished.

(C.) Hedge-and-back. Diagram 2-8 shows the same situation as the dribbler picking the ball up under the duress of a "jump." This situation occurs frequently after the dribbler has been trapped a few times. X3 races a few steps toward 1 (hedge) but recovers quickly back to an attacker in his lane. X3's hands are up forcing a lob or bounce pass that an alert X5 can anticipate. If X1 picks his dribble up, three defenders have the downcourt passing lanes and X5 is still at safety. X1 then harasses 1, yelling "used." If 1 keeps his dribble alive, the hedge-and-back has created doubt in 1's mind for future defensive moves, and the hedge-and-back has run some of the ten seconds off the clock. The dribbler still has to attack the basic slides of the 2-2-1 zone press.

(D.) Peel-back. Diagram 2-9 demonstrates the peel-back. X3 appears to be giving the outside lane to 1, as X3 does in the basic slide. X2,

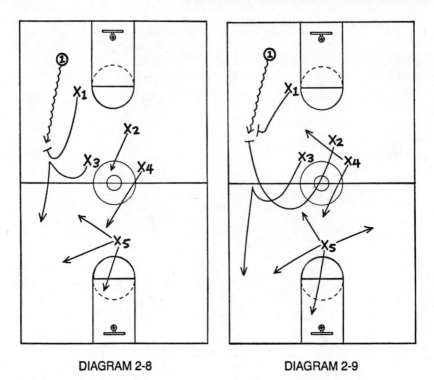

DIAGRAM 2-8   DIAGRAM 2-9

meanwhile, has dropped far above the advancement of the ball. At a surprise moment X2 peels back to cut off 1's drive. X1 double-teams. X4 covers the diagonal and horizontal passing lanes, and X3 covers the vertical and diagonal passing lanes. X5 plays safety. On a throwback pass, X4 moves up to help X1 on the front line. X5 and X2 mans the second line and X3 becomes the safety. If X5 did not have the skills to play the second line, X2 must race hard to cover the left second line. X3 would be X2's helpmate, and X5 would play safety. Coach Denny Crum's Louisville Cardinals used the peel-back beautifully in their drive for an NCAA National Championship.

(E.) *Give-outside—then-take-it-away.* Diagram 2-10 describes the peel-back's complement, the give-outside—take-it-away maneuver. X1 pressures 1, and X3 again shows 1 the open lane. In fact X3 retreats too deep to recover. This gives 1 the idea to drive hard as he does in the peel-back. At the proper moment, X1 cuts off 1; as 1 reverses, X2 traps with X1. X3 has vertical and diagonal passing lanes, and X4 has horizontal and diagonal. X5 plays safety. The horizontal passing lane was open initially in the peel-back, but is never open in the give-outside—take-it-away. The diagonal passing lane was closed completely in the peel-back, but it is open momentarily in the give-outside—take-it-away. These two complement each other.

(F.) Throwbacks. Whenever you plan to trap the thrown-in pass, to run the peel-back, to activate the give-outside—take-it-away, you must have a throwback rule or concede you will use only one trap in your press. Diagram 2-11 illustrates a throwback from these three defensive strategies. Player 1 makes a throwback pass to 2. X4 contains 2 while the others rotate. There are two ways you can rotate. You can stay with your 2-2-1 press by having X3 go hard to secondary left line coverage, giving X1 and X4 front line coverage. You could rotate X5, if he is capable, to left offensive secondary line coverage, X3 as safety, and X2 drop to right secondary coverage. Or you could abandon your 2-2-1 coverage and go to a 1-2-1-1 zone press. X4 would contain 2 until X1 arrives to trap. X3 and X2 would be rovers, racing to passing lanes. X3 gaps the vertical and diagonal lanes and X2 waits in the horizontal and diagonal lanes. X5 would stay at safety. A throwback from 2 back to 1 would have the defenders retracing their steps into the coverage of Diagram 2-11.

Diagram 2-11 can also demonstrate a long throwback pass and its defensive coverage. Many defensive teams will retreat immediately to half-court defense, believing that long throwbacks break their press. Player 1's pass to 4 would be a long throwback because the receiver is behind the first gap shooter. The more conservative defensive teams will

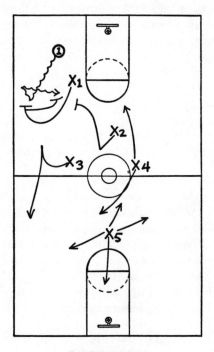

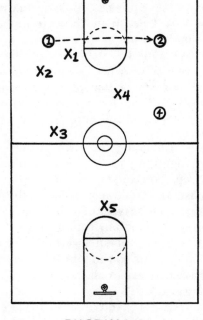

DIAGRAM 2-10   DIAGRAM 2-11

retreat to half-court but another trap can take place. To trap the long throwbacks, your team must have excellent overall speed. X3 would come over to channel 4 outside. X4 hurries to help X3 trap 4. X5 covers the vertical passing lane, leaving safety only when he sees X2 has recovered. X2 plays safety, and X1 covers the diagonal passing lane and shades the horizontal. Both X1 and X2 must hustle while the pass is in the air. All must have excellent speed and quickness.

Combining Slides to Reduce Offensive Efficiency. There are coaches who are great teachers of the game. Everything they need to teach a multiple 2-2-1 press has been given to them. Then there are great bench coaches—coaches who, during game situations, recognize what the opposition is doing and what they must do to combat it. There are few coaches who do both well. This section deals with the game (bench) coaching.

The basic slide (Diagram 2-2) leaves open momentarily the vertical passing lane, but the peel-back (Diagram 2-9) and the give-outside—take-it-away (Diagram 2-10) never open the vertical passing lane. A team throwing passes there can be stymied by the latter two stunts. Maybe you want to force the ball down the vertical passing lane. You can do this by the hedge-and-back (Diagram 2-8) or the run-and-jump (Diagram 2-6). You can allow vertical pass, encourage, or impel these passes, but before you enter the game you should have planned and drilled your athletes on these sequences. In fact, you can force, encourage, or allow any pass in any lane. With these techniques, you can take your opponents completely out of their full-court game. Many teams practice their full-court game less than they practice their half-court game. You are the master of your team's winning or losing.

It may be that your opponents cannot get the ball inbounds. You may want to deny or face-guard (see explanations at beginning of this chapter). You still have "off," which will change the pace of your press.

Changing the Pace of the 2-2-1 Press. There are many ways to change the pace of the 2-2-1 basic press. You could run-and-jump or "trap." You could face-guard or deny and immediately trap the inbounds pass. You could have rules on throwbacks that let you trap immediately again. These types of techniques would speed up the game. Or you could slow the tempo by running only the basic slides or the hedge-and-back.

The great equalizer of all the moves in the 2-2-1 zone press is "off." "Off" allows you to run the press the entire game without giving up a basket. It makes all the "ons," including basic, more effective once you discard "off."

In "off," you always want to cut the ball to the center of the court (funnel). X1 and X2 (see Diagram 2-1) must always keep the ball in front of them. Either X1 or X2 covers the ball and the other one drops to protect the middle. No two defenders ever double-team: They play it safe and "off." If the ball is passed from one guard area to the other (a horizontal pass), the opposite guard comes up and the original ball defender drops to protect the middle. If the ball is dribbled from one guard area toward the other, X1 and X2 can switch, can stay with the dribbler, or can run-and-jump. The three back defenders deny the pass to any player in their area. If a pass should penetrate the front two, those two defenders race upcourt until they are again ahead of the ball. You can keep the forward coverage on the new receiver and let the guard on the ball side drop to the second line of defense and the guard opposite the ball drop to his regular middle lane coverage (as in invert, Diagram 2-5). If two potential receivers overload any downcourt area, the defender responsible for that area must deny the front man the ball. The unoccupied area's defender must sag toward the overloaded area and help. The deepest defender floats like a free safety would in football. He can come as far upcourt as the last attacker, but he must be alert to any downcourt break. When the ball reaches beyond the second line of defense, this safety must retreat to the basket, giving up the ten-feet jumper but never the layup.

Adjustments. Adjustments take two forms: You can change basic slides and traps or you can change the entire objective of your press. As an example of an adjustment in basic slides, let's say you taught Diagram 2-2 as your basic slide; then Diagram 2-3 would be an adjustment. You can make these adjustments from game to game, but you should never try to make an untutored sliding or trapping adjustment during a game. Players could never react instinctively to such adjustments.

Diagram 2-12 offers an example of a planned adjustment. Let's say you intend to pressure after made free throws, but you want something a little different but stay with a 2-2-1 after the ball is inbounded. X1 and X2 double-team the out-of-bounds passer. X3 and X4 cover the first two inbounds receivers. X5 plays safety. Once the ball is inbounded, the defenders drop above the ball and run a planned 2-2-1 stunt.

Adjustments in your basics must be simple. They must supplement what you have already taught, and they must be practiced before you throw them into game situations.

THE 2-1-2 ZONE PRESS

Personnel Needed for the 2-1-2 Zone Press. Diagram 2-13 shows the initial alignment of a 2-1-2 zone press. Who plays the various positions depends on the skills of your squad members and what you want to get from your press.

If you intend to face-guard or deny the inbounds pass, your two quickest defenders, probably your guards, would occupy X1 and X2. X1 would cover the first attacker left and X2 would defend the first attacker right. These two defenders want to force the overhead lob, the slow

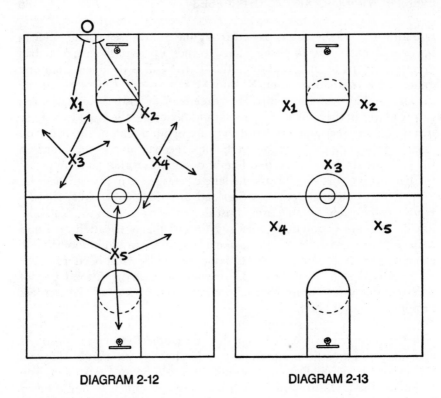

DIAGRAM 2-12   DIAGRAM 2-13

bounce pass, or the five-second count. They have to cover the receivers only for about three seconds. These two defenders would cover these cutters if they moved downcourt toward the midcourt line, but they drop their coverage about the 28-foot mark. Any longer pass X4 and X5 should intercept. These two defenders study the eyes and arms of the men they guard for any clue when the ball may be passed. A pass to their man results in a trap, a stunt, or some team technique being called. A pass opposite them calls for passing lane coverage. X3 should be your best athlete, your smartest basketball player. X3 must deflect lob passes to X1 and X2's men. X3 covers the third attacker trying to receive the inbounds pass. He may have to trap with X1 or X2; he may have to cover a passing lane if he is not involved in a trap. X4 and X5, when denying, are your weakest defenders. They coordinate their movement, like two men on a string. If X5 has to take a fourth cutter to the inbounds pass, X4 would drop deep. If X4 goes for a backcourt passing lane, X5 would cover deep. If the ball comes in on the left side of the court, X5 goes deep and X4 covers his vertical passing lane. A ball entering the right side would leave X5 in the vertical passing lane and X4 dropping deep.

If you decide to run only the basic slides and traps of the 2-1-2 zone press, you might want X1 and X2 as your forwards. X3 would be the center if he were agile enough to trap. X4 and X5 could be your quickest players. This would be your best alignment if you intended constantly to shoot the gaps for steals.

If you intended to run the "stunts" or to force the ball down the sidelines to midcourt before trapping, then X1, X2, and X3 should be your quicker, more agile, probably smaller defenders. If you used X4 and X5 to trap at midcourt (Diagram 2-15), they can be your slower defenders, but X3 must again be your best athlete.

Duties of Each Position. Duties change as objectives change. This year you might want one objective; next year you might alter the purpose of your press because the change best suits the personnel. Because all stunts, slides, and strategies receive maximum treatment, duties will be discussed as each individual section develops.

What the 2-1-2 Press Can Accomplish. The 2-1-2 full-court zone press is every bit as versatile as the 2-2-1, but it has never been as popular. When you have five quick defenders, you can face-guard, trap and run all the stunts and adjustments and even alternate the basic slides. If your personnel includes only three quick people, you can place them as X1, X2, and X3, and you can put your slower defenders as X4 and X5. With only three quick players, let X1, X2, and X3 stunt, trap and adjust, and let X4 and X5 work in unison on the back line. However, if you have only two quick defenders, discard any plans of denying the inbound pass, stunting, or trapping in backcourt. You would want to fan the ball outside, drive it up the sidelines, and trap it around midcourt. This takes advantage of your quickness and minimizes your weakness in your slower personnel.

The 2-1-2 is more for interceptions than the 2-2-1. You can use the 2-1-2 to speed up your opponent's attack, and you can use it to slow the tempo down.

What the 2-1-2 Press Cannot Do. The 2-1-2 full-court zone press runs the spectrum: It can accomplish whatever you design it to accomplish. If you use three slow and two quick players, it cannot force opponents to speed up play. But if you have five quick demons, it would accomplish anything you desire from face-guarding to primary and secondary traps and stunts. Most coaches, however, use man-to-man pressure when they have five quick players. In other words, the limits of the 2-1-2 zone press depends entirely on your personnel and the objectives of your press.

Where and When to Use the 2-1-2 Press. You can make the 2-1-2 press as safe as the 2-2-1 (see Diagram 2-14), or you can make it a mad, scrambling, panic-provoking press. Therefore, when you have the best of personnel, you could safely use the 2-1-2 for the entire game, reducing your opponents' effectiveness and adaptabilities by switching stunts and strategies periodically. When you have the worst of personnel—three slow and two quick—you could pick spots to apply it as a change of pace. With less than two quick defenders, you should choose another press. Just as you would not expect the worst of personnel to use the 2-1-2 to come from behind late in a game, you could expect the best of personnel to win many games in the opening minutes of play.

Basic Slides of the 2-1-2 Zone Press. There are two basic ways you can cover dribbles fanned to the outside, as shown in Diagrams 2-14 and 2-15. If you are a conservative presser or if your personnel demands conservatism, Diagram 2-14 is your answer. X1 compels 1 to dribble down the sidelines. X4 encourages 1 by showing an open lane. X4 drops before returning to set the trap with X1 near midcourt, as X3 did in the basic slides of the 2-2-1 (Diagrams 2-2 and 2-3). X3, who must be a good athlete with above-average speed and quickness, covers the vertical passing lane and shades the diagonal passing lane. X2 covers the horizontal passing lane and shades the diagonal. X5 drops to the free throw line to play safety.

Diagram 2-15 is for you if you want to gamble more. All five players in the 2-1-2 press must be quick and anticipate well. Diagram 2-15 could also be called the peel-back, although it is a basic slide of the 2-1-2 press. X1 pushes 1 outside, using aggressive one-on-one play. X3 is above the ball. When X3 sees an advantage he peels back to trap with X1. X2 covers

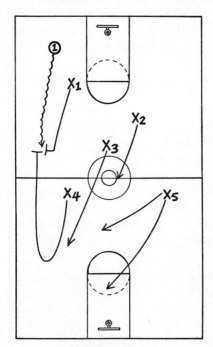

DIAGRAM 2-14

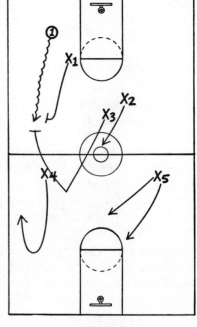

DIAGRAM 2-15

the horizontal passing lane, shading the diagonal. X5 drops to the free throw line and plays safety. X4 drops to let 1 "see" an open lane; then X4 covers the vertical lane, shading the diagonal.

You can use the slides of Diagram 2-15 if you intend to face-guard and then trap the successful inbounded pass. Diagram 2-15 permits an immediate trap even if you do not use denial.

Alternate Slides of the 2-1-2 Press. Diagram 2-16 suggests an alternate method of covering a quick trap of a successful inbounds pass. X3 needs to be your best athlete in both basic slides, but this alternate method of trapping the inbounds pass eliminates this requirement for X3. In fact, X3, X4, and X5 can all be slow and still recover adequately. X1 and X2, however, must possess quickness. X1 and X2 trap the ball. X3 is already in the horizontal and diagonal passing lanes, and X4 maintains his coverage in the vertical passing lane. X5 can drop quickly to become a safety; or because the trap is deep in backcourt, X5 can cover the diagonal passing lane as high as midcourt. It would be very difficult for 1 to find a receiver open deep.

Unlike the 2-2-1 press, the 2-1-2 has spots available for a secondary trap. There is even a place where you could activate a third trap. Also, all the stunts and mechanisms that follow can be added to your basic slide to

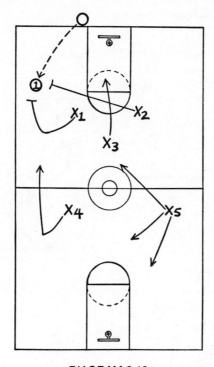

DIAGRAM 2-16

make your trapping 2-1-2 as multiple or as simple as you wish. The only requirement: Most of your defenders must be quick to handle these slides effectively.

(A.) Secondary trapping areas. To explain Diagram 2-17, let's begin with Diagram 2-15. In Diagram 2-15, X1 and X3 trap. If 1 passes to 2, that is a throwback pass and will be discussed later in this chapter. But sometimes 1 passes vertically, let's say to 4. X4 covers 4, keeping 4 from finding an open man quickly and giving X1, X2, X3, and X5 opportunity to complete the rotations they began while the pass was in flight. X3 traps with X4. X5 rotates to the vertical passing lane, but he does not leave the area of the basket until he sees X2 can arrive. X1 rotates to the horizontal passing lane while shading the diagonal lane. X2 plays safety.

A third trapping area is also available, but it is dangerous unless X1 and X2 can adequately defend a low-post attacker (Diagram 2-18). From Diagram 2-17, X4 and X3 trap the ball handler, 4. Then 4 passes to 5. X5 covers the vertical passing lane in Diagram 2-17. X5 now arrives to 5 when the ball arrives. X4 traps with X5. X2 sags to the low-post area. X2 must front any player there. X1 covers the weak side. X3 covers the high-post strong side.

If possession of the ball is a must, you could alter these passing lane coverages. X3 could cover the vertical pass back out of the corner, and X1

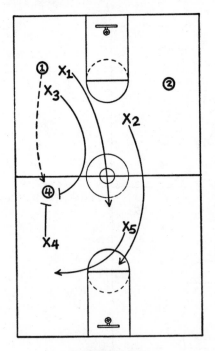

DIAGRAM 2-17

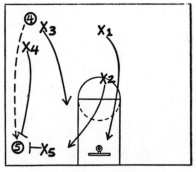

DIAGRAM 2-18

could cover the diagonally high-post passing lane. This would leave the weak side open. This option should be used sparingly, such as late in a game when you are down a point or two. In using this stunt, X5 must prevent a shot by 5. There is no defensive rebounder in the primary rebound area.

This third trapping area is also available when employing the 2-2-1 press. Using Diagram 2-2 as a beginning, a pass into the corner is covered by X5. X5 and X3 trap. X4 covers the low post, fronting any attacker who breaks there. X2 covers weak side, and X1 plays in the diagonal passing lane at the high post.

Some teams, especially when they are face-guarding, will throw a long pass from out-of-bounds to near midcourt in the vacuum between X1 and X4 (Diagram 2-13). This pass would receive the same trap and slide coverages illustrated by Diagram 2-17.

(B.) Run-and-jump. You should never trap in the middle lane while employing the 2-1-2 press. The holes are too many and the slides too long to permit adequate coverage. The run-and-jump opportunities to the middle are exceptional. Run-and-jumps to the outside are unadvisable.

Diagram 2-19 demonstrates the three-on-two run-and-jump drill explained in chapter 1 (Diagram 1-17). X1 funnels 1 to the middle, a change-up from the basic slides of the 2-1-2 press. X2 races at 1's dribble hand. X2 yells "jump." Meanwhile X3 has shot the gap on the "habit" pass to 2. X1 now exchanges duties with X3. X5 and X4 both drift with the progress of the dribbler: X5 into the backcourt vertical passing lane and X4 to safety. A pass from 1 to 2 could continue the run-and-jump, or X3 could force the ball down the sideline, activating the basic slide of Diagram 2-15 or another stunt.

(C.) Hedge-and-back. Hedge-and-back defensive moves eliminate the dribble without a double-teaming trap (Diagram 2-20). X1 pushes 1 up the sideline. X4 makes 1 think he is coming to help X1 trap. Player 1 picks up his dribble. X1 blankets 1, refusing to allow 1 vision downcourt. X4 hustles back to cover the vertical passing lane. X3 has diagonal short coverage. X2 covers the horizontal passing lane. X5 plays safety, defending the long lob pass and the basket area. Hedge-and-back permits pressure on the ball, yet it allows all three passing lanes to be covered and still maintain a safety.

(D.) Peel-back. Although Diagram 2-15 displays a basic slide of the 2-1-2 full-court zone press, it could also represent the peel-back. Technically, you could alter Diagram 2-15 into a different type of peel-back coverage. You could allow X2 to peel-back and trap with X1. X3 would then have horizontal and diagonal passing lane coverage. X4 keeps vertical and diagonal coverage, and X5 defends the basket area. In this coverage, only X2 and X3 exchange duties. This peel-back protects the

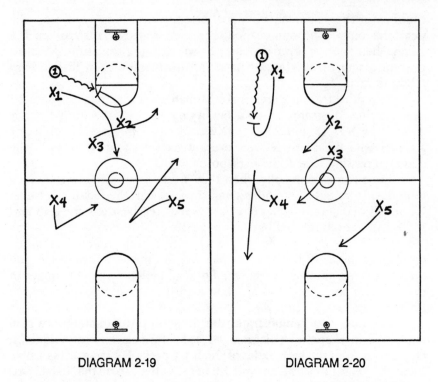

DIAGRAM 2-19   DIAGRAM 2-20

diagonal lane better than the peel-back of Diagram 2-15. Both could be taught; one as a change-up for the other.

(E.) *Give-outside—take-it-away.* Diagram 2-21 depicts the give-out-side—take-it-away. X1 channels 1 outside. X4 floats, letting 1 "see" the open lane. Player 1 begins to dribble hard. X1 cuts 1 off, forcing a reverse move back to the middle, or 1 must charge, or 1 must kill his dribble. If 1 picks up his dribble, X1 calls "used," activating the hedge-and-back (Diagram 2-20). Player 1 will usually reverse, and X2 arrives just as 1 comes out of the reverse. X1 and X2 trap. X3 covers the horizontal and diagonal passing lanes, and X4 blankets the vertical and diagonal lanes. X5 retreats to the free throw line to defend the basket area.

(F.) *Throwbacks.* The 2-1-2, like the 1-2-1-1, was made for excellent coverage of throwback passes. You could call the throwback coverage a three-man press with two deep defenders acting in unison. As the ball moves from 1 to 2, X5 comes to vertical lane coverage and X4 is pulled to safety coverage at the free throw line (Diagram 2-22). If the pass originally had gone down the vertical lane from 1 to 4, defenders would have covered as in Diagram 2-17. But that is an attacking pass, and this section deals with throwback passes. As the ball flies from 1 to 2, X2 arrives as 2 receives the pass. X2 must detain 2, forcing 2 to think over

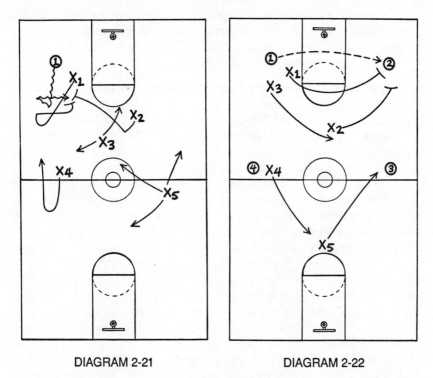

DIAGRAM 2-21   DIAGRAM 2-22

his next move. Meanwhile X1 comes to trap with X2. X3 drops to diagonal and horizontal passing lane responsibilities. A throwback from 2 to 1 would result in defenders reassuming the positions of Diagram 2-22.

If you are running one of the stunts without X3 trapping, have X2, X1, and X3 exchange duties. It is probably easier understood when you rule throwback coverages. A rule that is always suffice: whoever locates in the diagonal lane contains the new pass receiver; whoever vertically traps becomes the new diagonal lane cover; whoever horizontally traps, traps horizontally again. This holds true throughout all zone-press short throwback coverages.

A completed pass from 1 to 3 represents a long throwback pass (Diagram 2-22). There are two acceptable methods of covering the long throwback. You could let X5 stop the progress of 3 while all other defenders retreat to their half-court defense. Or you could rule a coverage for all long throwback passes. X5 cuts 3 outside while X2 comes quickly to help X5 trap 3. X4 takes the vertical passing lane, leaving the basket area only after he knows X3 can recover. X3 defends the basket area. X1 blankets the diagonal passing lane while being aware of a horizontal pass.

Offensive teams who do not attack the basket after breaking a press should always face secondary traps, the long throwback being an example. Only defensive teams with excellent speed and quickness should consider trapping long throwbacks.

Combining Slides to Reduce Offensive Efficiency. What some options give, others take away: the basic slide of Diagram 2-14 gives the vertical lane, but Diagram 2-15 takes it away. Your other consideration: How many people do you have who can press? You can run the 2-1-2 zone press with two quick pressers (the worst), or three (excellent) or five (the best). Your options are limited by the numbers you have.

If you choose to use only the slides, stunts, and adjustments of the 2-1-2, your team's success rests not only on your evaluation of your personnel and your opponent's personnel, but also on the combination of slides you choose to teach for a single game. Let's say you have the material to run Diagram 2-15 as your basic; then Diagrams 2-17 and 2-18 are your second and third traps. You can confuse your opponents by adding stunts. Use the Run-and-jump (Diagram 2-19) whenever the dribbler attacks the middle of the court. Hedge-and-back (Diagram 2-20) looks so much like the trap of Diagram 2-15, but this stunt completely closes the diagonal lane. The peel-back and give-outside—take-it-away leaves open the horizontal lane. Too many passes there can result in X3 shooting that gap. You could run your basic slide (Diagram 2-15) which closes the horizontal lane completely. Throwback passes result in continuous traps, or you can adjust your throwback into a complete press itself (three men trapping and two in unison).

The options are there for you to make a complete pressing system out of the 2-1-2, but you must recognize which part will work best at a particular moment during a game. Evaluate what your opponents are doing and choose the defensive option which closes that offensive option. Winning coaches are bench coaches as well as practice coaches. If, from scouting, you know your opponent's offense prior to game time, you can plan adjustments and have them ready. You do not have to recognize when you have excellent scouting reports. Do most of your bench coaching prior to game time. The defense has the advantage: You can make more adjustments than any team can learn offensive options.

Changing the Pace of the 2-1-2 Press. You can change the pace of the press in three ways. You can run slides designed to trap near midcourt. This slows down the offense. Or you can run stunts, along with face-guard or denial, that will pick up the tempo of the game. If you are behind late in a game, you would want stunts that are designed to force violations or steals.

"Off" offers a third way to control tempo. "Off" helps "on" after "off" has been used for a few possessions, regardless of which "on" you intend to run. X1 and X2 (Diagram 2-13) must stay ahead of the ball.

They will always want to funnel the dribbler. One of those two defenders cover the ball; the other drops to the middle, hedging at the dribbler, putting a doubt in his mind. This is especially effective after you have run-and-jumped a few times. When in "off," you never double-team trap. A pass from one guard area to the other is met with X1 and X2 exchanging duties. A dribble from one guard area to another allows the defense to "jump," to switch, or it allows the defender on the dribbler to stay. The three back defenders deny anyone in their area the flash pivot or a direct pass. If a pass is successful over the front two, everyone must race ahead of the ball. If two potential receivers overload a downcourt area, the defender in that area takes an attacker closer to the ball. The downcourt defender without a man in his area sags to the middle until he finds the deepest man he must cover. Guards must pressure the ball or a good passer will easily find this open downcourt receiver. X4 and X5 must act as though they are on a string. A ball on X1's side of the court would find X4 up in a vertical passing lane and X5 as a free safety deep at the free throw line. This free safety roams deep. X3 drops for diagonal pass coverage. A ball passed from one side of the court to the other has X5 pulling high and X4 dropping to roam with X3 hunting the open diagonal receiver. This gives the appearance of a zone press but there will be no trap. A pass covered by X3 in the middle of the court could result in a change of duties. If the pass started from X2, X1 would drop and become the new X3, for example. This maintains pressure on the ball, and it allows for "off" to continue the zone look.

"Off" slows the tempo of the game tremendously. Whenever you activate an "on" stunt which speeds up the game, few offensive teams can adjust to it.

Adjustments. There are two ways you can adjust. You can change slides to counteract an opponent's offense, or you can change the entire objective of your press.

Coaches who have used the 2-1-2 zone press say they have effectively adjusted by trapping location of the ball. If the pass is inbounded in front of the guards, you trap with X1 and X2 (Diagram 2-16). If it is entered behind X1 and X2 but not near midcourt, you trap with X1 and X3 (Diagram 2-15). If it is lobbed near midcourt, you trap with X1 and X4 (Diagram 2-14). You could in this last option use Diagram 2-17 and trap with X3 and X4. This adjustment would not force teaching new slides because the players would already know Diagrams 2-14, 2-15, 2-16, and 2-17. You could still face-guard, or you could let your opponents throw the pass inbounds anywhere they wish. Or you could think up any slide or diagram that best suits your personnel for a change of pace.

Diagram 2-23 offers yet another adjustment by a defensive team that has absolutely no team speed. You would want to use the midcourt line as an extra defender. Force the ball up the sideline; it doesn't matter if the ball gets there by pass or by dribble. X1 and X3 would trap. There can be no backward pass—that is a violation. X4 stays in the vertical lane. X2 covers the short diagonal lane and shades the horizontal lane. X5 retreats to the free throw line area as safety. With no team speed you would not want a second trap. You would want to retreat near the basket and hide your lack of speed.

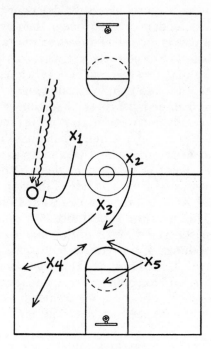

DIAGRAM 2-23

3

Odd Front
Full-Court Zone Presses

Odd front presses consists of one defender or three defenders on the front line. Both the diamond press (1-2-1-1 and its variation the 3-1-1) and the jug press (1-2-2 and its variation the 3-2) are very versatile, but both require above-average quickness. The diamond press along with the box press (see chapter 2) have the largest following among basketball coaches.

Both the diamond and the jug will receive elaborate treatment in this chapter. Their variations, adjustments, stunts, and strategies will also be explained from the three-defender front.

THE DIAMOND PRESS (1-2-1-1) AND ITS VARIATION (3-1-1)

To change the diamond press to its variation, you merely take the defender on the out-of-bounds passer and drop him to the free throw line. There are many reasons, other than personnel, that might prompt you to consider this adjustment. You may want to use short-stopping techniques, or your may want to guide the inbounds pass to the most favorable defensive floor position. The offensive pattern might have its primary receivers in the middle near the free throw line. You might wish to allow the ball inbounds and trap immediately with a wing and the middle man of the three-man front. Also, you may not have the personnel to go 1-2-1-1.

Before explaining the personnel types needed to make a 1-2-1-1 or 3-1-1 press effective, you need to understand the trapping areas of the diamond press. All diamond presses trap in Area I (Diagram 3-1). Area I allows for two gap shooters and one safety, or it permits three gambling gap shooters. Area I also allows excellent trapping of the throwback passes with both types of downcourt lane coverage. If you have average or above-average quickness, you can design a secondary trap in Area II. A third trap is possible in Area III if you have superior quickness. Both Areas II and III should cover the lanes with two gap shooters and a safety. Even this lane coverage can be altered if you feel you are that much superior.

First look where the holes of this zone press appear (Diagram 3-2). In Area II near midcourt, there is a hole on each side of the court. A pass from out-of-bounds to receivers stationed there would defeat your press. So you must have a method of moving either wingmen X2 or X3 back to help X4 (diamond); or you could bring X5 up to help X4 (that is the jug press). Different type personnel would dictate which type is best for you to use.

It would be defensive suicide for you to use three defenders (X1, X2, X3) in Area I when there are only two attackers there. You would

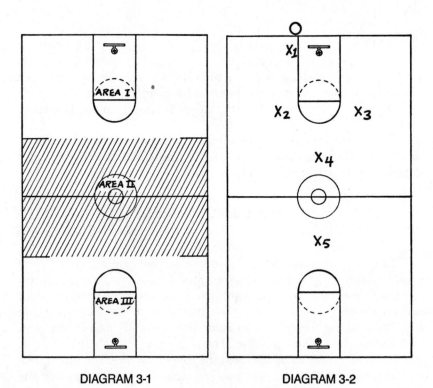

DIAGRAM 3-1   DIAGRAM 3-2

want to force three attackers up to Area I by shortstopping or some defensive technique to impel another attacker to come from Area II into Area I to receive the inbounds pass.

It is equally offensive suicide to throw an inbounds pass all the way to Area III. X5 should intercept. You may want to bring X5 to midcourt to help X4 if the offense brings a fifth man into backcourt (this is the jug—see later section in this chapter). You can definitely bring X5 near midcourt on effective traps set in Area I. In fact, it is often safe to bring X5 completely into backcourt on excellent traps in Area I, especially if X5 has excellent quickness.

Characteristics for Personnel of the Diamond Press. What you intend to accomplish determines where you will station your personnel. You undoubtedly have good team quickness or you would not consider this press. So, face-guarding and denial become your first considerations. X1 can be a big player, either a center or a forward. He can have great or average quickness, but he must be aggressive. He wants to get on the out-of-bounds passer, getting as close to the out-of-bounds line as he can without touching it. He wants to jump up and down, yell, distract, pressure hard the out-of-bounds passer (Diagram 3-3). If X1 can deflect a pass from 1 back out-of-bounds, he should. This adds twofold to the

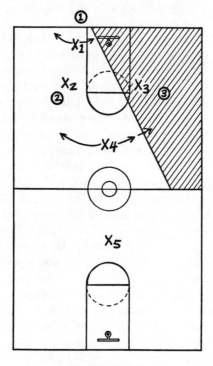

DIAGRAM 3-3

defense: It makes 1 more cautious on his next passes, and it restricts the movement of the passer. On a violation the player throwing the ball inbounds cannot run the baseline. Any movement by 1's pivot foot would constitute a walk. X1 can even use shading techniques. He has two options. He can play on 1's left closing off the complete shaded area (Diagram 3-3) of the court. He does this if X2 can handle 2. This also frees X4 to concentrate on entry passes to his left. Or X1 can shade 1's right. This helps X2 and it also helps X3. Because of X1's positioning of his body, no chest pass can be thrown to 2. So X2 can deflect a bounce pass or X4 can help on the lob. X3 plays denial instead of face-guard because X3 has the backboard to help him. Player 1 cannot throw lob to 3 without hitting the backboard. X4 knows this and shades toward 2. X2 deflects any bounce pass or chest pass directed toward 3. If 1 runs the baseline, legal only after score, X4 must make X2 and X3 aware of the change. This means the shading occurs on the other side. X4 merely calls left or right. When a lob pass is thrown inbounds, X4 yells "ball."

You could, if you prefer, drop X1 to the free throw line. But now X1 must have quick hands, good speed, excellent reflexes, and lots of savvy. This also frees 1 of pressure, but it gains you another defender in the heart of the reception area. X1 could shortstop with either X2 or X3, forcing a pass into a second best receiver. Your alignment is now a 3-1-1 face-guard.

In either face-guard alignment, X2 and X3 need to be tall but agile. Quickness is more important than height while face-guarding, but once the ball has been inbounded, height becomes more important than quickness. This forces a higher lob out of a double-team trap. It also helps if these two anticipate lanes well. They will play in passing lanes when on the weak side. These two must also be adapt at containing a dribbler before applying the trap. X4, the short safety in both the diamond and the 3-1-1, must possess quickness and speed. He must be your best anticipator, and he must be your best athlete. X5 either can be slow or he can be quick. If you have a slow, big defender who jumps and protects the basket well, this could be his spot. If X5 is exceptionally quick, tall, agile, and fast, you would do better with the jug (1-2-2) press. If you have three quick defenders (X2, X3, X4), you can face-guard press. Four or five quick defenders makes your press that much better.

You can get by with less than three, but you would not want to face-guard. You could deny the ball to one side of the court and permit entry on the other side. This allows for specialization: each player would perform the same task on every possession. You might not wish to defend throwback passes when specializing. You might want to gamble once then retreat. From either the diamond or the 3-1-1, you could allow X3, for example, to be quick (Diagram 3-3). X3 would deny 3 an entry pass. X2 lets 2 receive the pass. X1 and X2 trap. X3 and X4, who must also be quick and fast, cover the passing lanes while X5 plays safety. This always has X1 and X2 trapping, X3 in the horizontal and diagonal passing lanes, and X4 in the vertical and diagonal passing lanes. This takes advantage of specialized skills. Should the offensive pattern be more effective going in on 2's side of the court, you could simply change 2 and 3's side. Now you still have the specialization, but you have disrupted the offensive schemes.

You could with great team quickness or without allow entry passes to either side, then-double team and play the passing lanes. In this case, X4 still must be your quickest and best athlete. X2 and X3 need to be agile and the bigger the better. X1 and X5 can be quick or slow, depending on what you expect them to do in your press. X1 needs to be quicker than X5 if you intend to trap throwback passes. X5 needs to be quicker if you intend to use X5 in your rotations.

Duties of Each Position. X1, the point on the 1-2-1-1 and the middle on the 3-1-1, always traps the inbounds pass in front of the wings, X2 and X3. The point and the wing should force the inbounds receiver to make a move before he is under control. To give this ball handler no time to plan is an objective of the odd zone presses. Before trapping the inbounds receiver, X1, if he is pressuring the out-of-bounds passer, steps back toward the middle and squares his shoulders to the ball, rather than go directly toward it. This is called "running the banana route". The wing trapper also plays middle to the outside. These two trap by bringing toes and knees together, backs straight, hands up in the plane of the ball but not reaching for the ball. They don't want to foul. They don't want to steal the ball from the receiver's hands. They want to steal his pass.

Before dribbling, the two trappers, the wing and the point, want to attack the ball handler to force him to start a dribble. If the dribbler is exceptionally fast and talented, the defenders do not want to attack. They should wait and let this dribbler come to the defense. Frequently an unsure or inexperienced dribbler will bounce the ball once and pick it up immediately when attacked. However, if he does not pick up his dribble but tries to escape by driving down the sideline, X4 can draw the charge as the dribbler turns the corner (see Diagram 3-4). If X4 cannot get to the corner to draw the charge it gives the wing a perfect chance to flick the dribble away. Let's say X1 and X2 trapped 2. Player 2 dribbles the sideline on X2 (Diagram 3-4). X4 has preliminary positioning in the vertical passing lane. X2 steps across the dribbler, rather than behind his outside leg; X2 slaps up at the dribble, being careful to avoid contact. This type of flicking does not work unless 2 has completely beaten X2. A flick to X4 will get X2 a pass back for a layup. There is a danger in teaching this flick. Although this situation occurs many times during a game and although the defensive players love it, it is not good fundamental defensive teamwork. It is a recovery from making a defensive

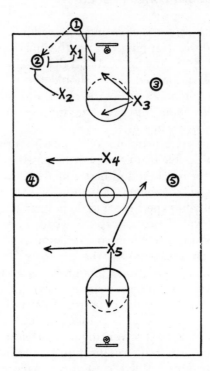

DIAGRAM 3-4

mistake, namely letting a dribbler escape a trap. Because players love it, it can lead to lazy trapping and stunting techniques.

Regardless of which side the entry pass comes onto the court, X4 covers the vertical passing lane and the opposite wing covers the horizontal passing lane. They both shade to the diagonal lane. X5 defends the basket unless he has speed and unless an excellent initial trap has been set. In this case X5 comes into frontcourt and covers the lob passes but shades the diagonal passing lane. It is difficult for an attacker who has been trapped ninety feet from his basket to find an open teammate above the midcourt line.

All the duties change on the next pass. If 2 passes to 1, 3, or 5, it represents a throwback coverage (see later in this chapter). If 2 passes to 4, it becomes a secondary trap (see later section). As those passes occur, we will explain the new responsibilities of each position.

What the Diamond Press Can Accomplish. It can increase the tempo of the game remarkably. It can bring your team from "definite" defeat to sudden and swift victory. It forces ball handlers to make mistakes. Steals frequently result in layups for your team, so it can be an offensive weapon. It can cause hurried jump shots, even when the press is broken. It can unnerve, even destroy, a patterned style ball club.

What the Diamond Press Cannot Do. It will not slow down the pace of the game. It will not result in safe play. Frequently steals, interceptions, and points come in bunches for your club; layups and short jump shots lay in wait for your attacking opponents. Unless you can tolerate a few easy baskets against your defense and unless you can sell your players on the idea that you'll get two for every one you give, you should run another press. Without this philosophy, your players will lose faith in your press. They won't attack. They'll become too cautious, and that will destroy your diamond press.

Where and When to Use the 1-2-1-1 Full-Court Press. You could use the diamond press any time as a surprise element, such as after successful free throws or for the last three minutes of a quarter. You can use it late in a game to try to overtake your opponents when your team is behind. This is probably the worst time to use it. You should not use it for an entire game unless you have built-in safety features, such as "off," or unless you want to double the possessions your opponents are accustomed to. If you ever face an opponent—and there are still a few— who will not attack the basket but wants only to get the ball across the timeline, you will lose nothing by pressing the entire game. And you will gain many steals and interceptions.

Basic Slides of the Diamond Press. Diagram 3-4 examines the basic slide in Area I of the diamond or the 3-1-1 full-court zone press. X1 traps 2 with X2. X1 cannot allow 2 to drive by him on the baseline; X2 cannot permit 2 to dribble by him up the sideline. Both will not permit dribble penetration down the middle. If the trap had occurred on the other side, X3 would assume X2's duties. X4 always covers the horizontal passing lane and shades the diagonal. The weakside wing, X3 in Diagram 3-4, covers the diagonal passing lane and shades the horizontal lane. X5 plays safety. If the trap by X1 and X2 is exceptional, or if gambling tactics are needed, such as late in the game and you are down considerably, X5 could come into backcourt and take the diagonal lane. X3 could gamble in the horizontal lane. Even if such strategy is not required, X3 could occasionally gamble in the horizontal lane.

Diagram 3-5 shows a secondary trapping area. Any time the pass is made to half-court, out of a trap or by inbounding, the new receiver, 4 in Diagram 3-5, must be forced to the sideline before another trap is considered. Diagram 3-5 illustrates the slides of a vertical pass. Diagram 3-9 exhibits the long throwback pass. It is considered a vertical pass if it is thrown vertically out of a trap or if it is thrown from out-of-bounds. X4 and X2 trap 4. X3 races hard to cover the diagonal passing lane as well as the basket area. When X5 sees X3 can reach his destination, X5 moves over to cover the vertical passing lane. If you don't want X5 in the rotation, X3 would have the vertical lane. X1 hustles to blanket the short diagonal lane and to shade the horizontal lane.

Diagram 3-6 exposes the third trapping area. This should not be attempted if you don't have superior quickness or if your philosophy does not consider constant pressure. X5 moves to the corner and halts 5's baseline drive. X4 hustles to stop the pass back out to forecourt. He can help X5 trap 5. X2 denies any pass into the high-post area, and X1 defends the weak side. X1 rebounds the weak side if a shot is taken by 5. X3 must front the low post.

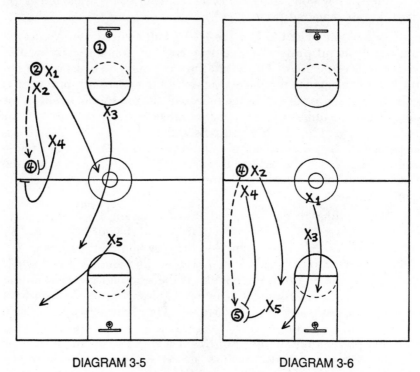

DIAGRAM 3-5   DIAGRAM 3-6

You could relinquish the safety features if you need the ball desperately, like late in a game when you are down by several points. In this case X3 could play the passing lanes vertically back out. X1 would then deny passes into the high post when gambling, and X5 must make sure 5 does not get off the shot. Otherwise your opponents would simply put back in a weakside rebound, and you have no defender there.

Alternate Slides of the Diamond Press. Diagram 3-7 shows an alternate slide to Diagram 3-4. Two conditions should unfold before using this alternate slide: X1 and X2 must have an effective trap in Area I, and X5 must possess speed and quickness. If your personnel can duplicate these requirements, your diamond press will intercept many more passes. Because X1 and X2 have trapped in Area I, it would be difficult for 2 to deliver an accurate pass into Area III even if he located an open teammate. X4 covers the vertical passing lane; X3 hovers just outside the horizontal lane; X5 defends the dangerous diagonal lane. X3 can help X5 in the diagonal lane if that is your preference.

Diagram 3-8 displays a safer alternative to Diagram 3-5. It is the safest alignment on traps in Area II because X5 never leaves the area of the basket. In this case, you would want X5 to be a shot blocker or intimidator. The pass can reach 4 from out-of-bounds as well as a vertical pass out of a trap. Regardless how the ball reaches 4, X4 must force 4 to the sideline and stop him while X2 comes to clamp the trap. X3 races to the vertical lane coverage, and X1 hustles to the horizontal lane coverage. They both shade the diagonal lane. X5 never leaves safety.

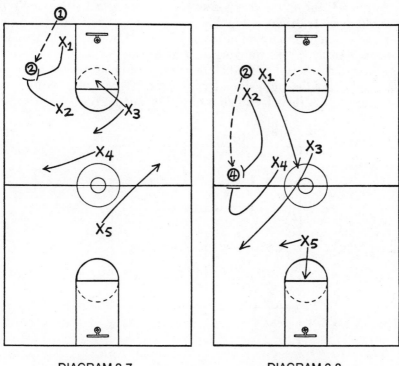

DIAGRAM 3-7   DIAGRAM 3-8

Diagonal passes out of the trap in Area I will defeat your diamond press. Whichever defender is responsible for the pass into the middle area must deny it, intercept it, or deflect it. A pass into this diagonal lane easily can be kicked out to the opposite lane and dribbled into forecourt. Traps in the middle lane do not exist from the diamond formation. The ball must be kept out of the middle.

Because the 1-2-1-1 tries to force quick action, the hedge-and-back has no place in your defensive scheme unless you want to run it while playing "off." The run-and-jump and the peel-back can work during "off." But it is best to consider the run-and-jump only as a stunt. Give-the-outside—take-it-away works on presses near midcourt. (Diagram 3-8, X4 impels 4 outside, takes it away and gets help from X2 for the trap.)

Throwbacks. The defensive coverage on throwbacks are perfect for the diamond press. In fact, throwbacks can be covered continuously in a structured form. Throwback coverage can be called a complete press within itself. There are three potential throwback passes against the diamond press: a pass to 1, a pass to 3, and a pass to 5 represent throwbacks (see Diagram 3-9). Each receives thorough treatment.

As 1 enters the pass into 2, you will recall X1 slides up the middle lane, squares himself to 2, then comes to set the trap with X2 (the banana route). This prevents 2's quick return pass to 1, and it allows X3 time to station himself for an interception of the pass back to 1 (Diagram 3-9). X3 would delay 1's dribble, should he receive a pass from 2, until X1 can cover 1 adequately. You would not want a trap on 1 by X3 and X1 because a pass to 3 easily breaks your press. It is best for X3 to delay 1, which stops the quick reversal of the ball. X3 delays 1 but shades his coverage on 3. X3 hedges the right shoulder of 1, and X1 retreats a step or two before he races at the left shoulder of 1, the banana route. X1 slows his

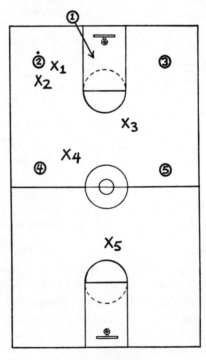

DIAGRAM 3-9

approach if 1 keeps his dribble alive. X1 must not let 1 drive the middle although both X2 and X3 are in perfect help position.

A pass from 2 to 3 typifies the short throwback described in chapter 1. Its reception occurs in front of X3. X3 cuts 3 outside, then takes the sideline away as he sees X1 arrive to help trap 3. X1 should sag as deep as the ball before coming over to help trap. X2 has the diagonal passing lane, shading the horizontal passing lane. X2 and X3 have merely exchanged duties. There are two coverages for X4 and X5. If you want X5 always to guard the basket area because of X5's characteristics and skills, X4 would have to run the width of the court and cover the vertical passing lane from 3 to 5. If X5 can enter the rotation, X5 would cover the vertical passing lanes, and X4 would sag to the spot midway between the free throw circle and the half-court circle.

A pass from 2 to 5 illustrates the long throwback pass, and this pass breaks your diamond press unless X5 can enter the rotations. X5 can pick off many of these crosscourt long diagonal passes if he anticipates well and if X1 and X2 have done their jobs. On this completed throwback, X5 cuts 5 to the sideline, brings him under control. X3 traps with X5. The remainder of the rotation depends on your team's quickness and your willingness to gamble. If you have excellent team quickness and your personality permits gambling, X4 would rotate to the vertical passing lane, X2 would cover the basket and the diagonal passing lane, and X1 would cover the horizontal receiver's lane. If you want a little more safety, let X4 go directly toward the basket area. Have X2 and X1 retreat quickly into frontcourt. If X2 could get to the vertical lane it would be his.

Combining Slides to Reduce Offensive Efficiency. The diamond press not only works well with its variation (3-1-1), but it also works miracles when combined with the jug press (1-2-2) and its variation (3-2). The diamond press advocate can begin his options by altering the slides that are available in the first half of this chapter with the slides that are presented in the second half of this chapter (more on this idea when we present the 1-2-2 parallel section).

A team having trouble inbounding the ball should meet face-guard or denial pressure. You could leave X1 on the out-of-bounds passer, or you could drop him to left field or shortstop, depending on which maneuver will help most.

A team that has initial trouble passing out of the first trap (Diagram 3-4) will soon solve the trap. You must find an alternate solution or disband your press for a few possessions. You have two options available: You could change your slides from Diagram 3-4 to Diagram 3-7, which would allow greater downcourt coverage on the first pass out of the trap, or you could seek a trap elsewhere. By seeking a trap elsewhere, you have two other options: You could force the ball to your secondary trapping area (Diagram 3-5 or Diagram 3-8), or you could force a dribble into the secondary trapping area. Diagram 3-10 shows how you can encourage this dribble. Once you get the dribble going, you have available the hedge-and-back, the run-and-jump, the peel-back, the give-the-out-side—take-it-away. All of these stunts will receive treatment when we discuss the 3-2 zone press later in this chapter. Because the 1-2-1-1, the 3-1-1, the 1-2-2, and 3-2 are so similar, any stunt which works for one will work for all.

You must evaluate what is happening during a game, and you must decide whether to abandon or change the slides of your press. Each particular slide while you double-team leaves an opponent open some-where. When your counterpart discovers that opening, you should close it by changing the slides. You should not abandon your press too early.

Changing the Pace of the Diamond Press. Diamond presses tend to speed up a ball game. To change its pace you could teach two presses, the diamond and the box. The box has as its objective to slow down attacks. Or you could teach the diamond thoroughly by teaching "off."

Stunts, discussed thoroughly later in this chapter, offer another method of changing the pace. Hedge-and-back, for example, will slow a dribble, but peel-back would halt it completely, forcing a pass.

"Off" remains the great equalizer. While in "off," you would want to funnel because all your "ons" involve fanning maneuvers. A ball in-bounded on the left defensive side would be covered by X2 (Diagram 3-3). X2 would force the dribbler to the inside or center of the court. X1 would not go to trap as he does in "on"; X1 would cover the out-of-bounds passer as he steps inbounds. Frequently offensive teams try to break the press by making a quick pass back to 1 as he steps inbounds. Should 1 cut through the press, X1 would follow as high as the free throw line or until he gets above the ball. Meanwhile X4 would slide into the vertical passing lane, and X3 would occupy a much deeper area than normal. X3 still patrols the middle lane but near midcourt as he would if you ran the box zone press.

X1 and X2 now want to keep the ball in front of them. A pass over their heads has them responding with a quick recovery ahead of the ball. A dribble would be run-and-jumped; if the dribbler escaped to the sideline X4 could "jump" with X2, leaving X4 and X1 as the front two.

Both defenders, originally X3 and X4, deny any man in their area the ball. They cover flash-pivots with man-to-man denial principles. Should a pass be successful, however, that defender stays with the new receiver. The front two have retreated on the pass to points above the ball. One of the front two replaces the original back defender, leaving the appearance of the box. If the pass were to X4's man, X2 would become the back defender; if the pass were to X3's man, X1 would become the back defender. X5 floats as a free safety would in football.

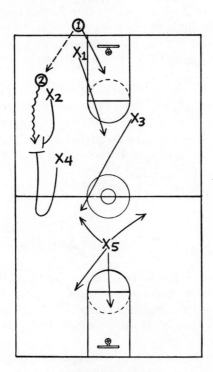

DIAGRAM 3-10

Where "on" fanned the ball and trapped to compel a pass, "off" funnelled the ball and forced the offense to move by dribble. This dribble movement opened up all the defensive stunts: the run-and-jump, the hedge-and-back, the peel-back, and the give-the-outside—take-it-away.

Adjustments. Two different type adjustments await the bench coach. You can alter the slides of your basic press, covering up an open area and opening up a covered area. Or you can change completely the objectives of your press. The first type adjustment was explained in the section on combining slides to reduce offensive efficiency. In this section, we will change the objectives of the press.

Diagram 3-10 displays the adjustments that lead to entirely new objectives for the diamond press. When 1 passes into 2, X1 stays man-to-man with 1, preventing the throwback pass to 1. If 1 cuts through the press, X1 would stop when he gets above 2. X1 would then deny any pass back to the middle. X1 now is playing off the ball instead of trapping with X2. X2 plays the ball handler on his inside shoulder. X2 can offer pressure, making 2 think it is a bad double-team, especially effective after X2 and X1 have trapped a few times. X2 must not pressure so tightly that 2 can drive between X2 and X4. X4 drops, letting 2 "see" the open outside lane. X2 now has two options: he can flick (as described in chapter 1), or he can direct the dribbler down the sideline. X4 can hurry back to near midcourt and run-and-jump. X3 could peel-back. X2 could give-outside—take-it-away. Or as shown in Diagram 3-10, X4 can hedge-and-back to trap with X2.

After the trap, which X4 and X2 would want to set as near midcourt as possible, X5, X3, and X1 have two rotations available. Their rotations depend upon the skills of X5. If X5 is agile and decently quick, X5 covers the vertical lane, X3 the diagonal lane and the basket area, and X1 hovers in the horizontal lane. If you do not want X5 in the rotation, but you want X5 near the basket, X3 gets the vertical lane, shading the diagonal, and X1 blankets the horizontal, shading the diagonal.

THE JUG PRESS (1-2-2)
AND ITS VARIATION (3-2)

Personnel Needed for the Jug and Its Variation. You will need five players with better than average quickness to make your jug press of championship caliber. You could possibly reduce the objectives of your press and use only four quick defenders, putting your slowest at X1 (Diagram 3-11).

X1 should be your center, your tallest player (Diagram 3-11). It is his responsibility to keep the ball out of the center lane. By being tall and active and by playing on the baseline as near the out-of-bounds passer as possible, X1 can force a high lob to the free throw lane area. Remember, X1 also has the backboard to help him. X1 wants to force the pass into the corners of the outside lane. If you choose to run the jug's variation, the 3-2, X1 would drop to the free throw line; but his duties would not change. X1 should follow the inbounds passer with his body. He should keep his hands high and active. This eliminates the direct pass, forcing the lob or the bounce. Both the bounce and the lob can receive harassment from X2 and X3.

X2 and X3 have virtually the same duties. The wing on the side of the ball traps with X1. The wing opposite the ball shades a passing lane. If your opponent attacks with right-handed dribblers, you should make X2 your best trapper; if a team has one or more left-handed dribblers, you should let X3 be your best trapper.

X4 and X5 need to be extremely quick and agile. They have the same duties. They both must cover any long pass from out-of-bounds. X1 helps by keeping his hands up and active. Once the ball is inbounded, the deep defender on the side of the ball will cover the vertical passing lane and the deep defender opposite the ball can cover deep or the diagonal passing lane.

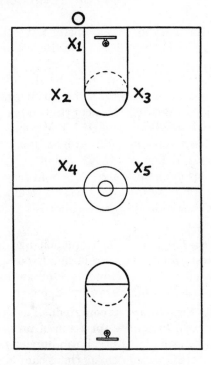

DIAGRAM 3-11

When you employ X1, X2, and X3 as your tallest defenders and X4 and X5 as your quick guards, you will usually allow the ball inbounds, then trap and cover the passing lanes. This also allows quick conversion from offensive rebounding into the press positions. It also has the guards deep, preventing a quick long pass from out-of-bounds.

You can run the jug and its variation by putting X1, X2, and X3 as your quickest players and X4 and X5 as your slowest. In this case you would want X1 to be the hustler, the best defensive player, like most point guards. X2 and X3 should have the same characteristics as X1, but taller. X4 and X5 would be your slowest players. From this placement of personnel, you could face-guard as well as run the quicker stunts: peel-back, run-and-jump, give-the-outside—take-it-away. Also from this placement, you might rather send the deep offside defender to cover the basket also. This reduces the number of backcourt defenders to four.

Face-Guard. While face-guarding the inbounds pass, X2 would take the first attacker cutting to the left side and X3 would deny the first attacker cutting to the right side. X1 can assume several different positions. If is best if X1 pressures the out-of-bounds passer. X1 should line up against the baseline, distracting the passer as best he can.

Together X1 and the backboard eliminate half of the court if the opponent decides to throw the ball in from the left or right side of the court. X1 must keep proper body positioning to accomplish this. For example, if the passer moves to his right, X1 shades the inside of the court. This eliminates the bounce and the direct pass because of X1's body to the right side of the defensive court. The backboard eliminates the lob. X3 can deny instead of face-guard. It also enables X4 to help X2 on a lob. X2 should ardently deny. X5 covers a flash pivot or goes deep.

X1 could drop and help, with X2 and X3, double-team a good inbounds ball handler (shortstopping). X1 could play leftfield, helping both X2 and X3 on lob passes. In this case, X1 would pick up the third cutter to the ball. You should designate either X4 or X5 to pick up the third cutter to the ball.

Duties of Each Position. The duties change according to the objectives of the press. You must keep in mind your personnel as they relate to the personnel of your opponents. Only in that dimension can you determine who will be your X1, your X2, etc.

What the Jug Press Can Accomplish. The jug press and its variation can accomplish the entire spectrum of press objectives. It can force a team to run by using its basics, it can impel a team into a slower tempo by executing "off," or it can create chaos running a team out of its patterns by employing any of its many stunts. The jug press can bring a team from far back to victory, or it can keep constant pressure on when it is ahead.

Because the jug uses five defenders in backcourt, it probably produces more turnovers than other backcourt presses. Unless two quick defenders occupy X4 and X5, it concedes more easy baskets than any of its kinships. Teams that use the jug press must be psychologically prepared not to let up when they give up easy baskets.

What the Jug Press Will Not Do. The jug cannot slow games down. It won't provide safety features unless you engage "off." If you are not an aggressive coach, you might do better with a safer press. Unless you can mentally train your personnel not to worry about a few layups, your team members will lose faith in the jug press. This loss of faith begins the defeat of your pressing system. Players become sluggish. They play with less aggressiveness and enthusiasm. More and more easy shots develop.

There are two ways you can teach frontcourt coverage on long passes (see Diagram 3-12). X1 and X2 trap 2, while X3, X4, and X5 are all in the backcourt covering passing lanes. The area near the basket is open. If X1 and X2 have done their jobs, 2 will never find the open basket area. However, if 2 lobs the ball vertically over X4's head you could have X5 race to cover the receiver. X4 would race to the basket area. A lob to the other side of the court would have X4 covering the receiver

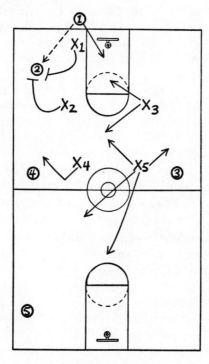

DIAGRAM 3-12

and X5 hustling to the basket area. You could rule that a pass over X4's head has X4 covering the receiver and X5 covering the basket. The former rule allows greater pressure in the backcourt and adequate downcourt coverage. In this case, X4 and X5 will not play as aggressively in the passing lanes in the backcourt. You must decide which of the two rules to follow. Don't teach both: This only confuses your own athletes.

Frequently, a short pass in front of X4 or X5 is followed by a quicker pass downcourt and an easy shot. The offside defender is responsible for this second pass. A gamble and a miss results in a layup. Often playing it safe ends in a two-on-one or three-on-one. This feature cannot be reduced from the jug press. Its aggressive backcourt nature more than rewards its employers.

Where and When to Use the Jug Press. You may use it any time during a game after a made free throw, a made field goal, or a violation on or near the baseline. You can use it too much. When a team adjusts to your lack of downcourt defense, it's best to go to a stunt, to "off," or to the relative safety of the 1-2-1-1. You simply adjust one of your back men to cover the basket area. You might even drop both defenders deeper. Only a deflection from the trap or an interception of the pass out of the trap will pay backcourt dividends. But the tandem duo, X4 and X5, will eliminate long passes, giving your press another look. This tandem duo, because of their quickness and speed, can gap frontcourt attackers, frequently stealing softly thrown or badly spotted passes.

You can alter the pressure before the pass is thrown inbounds. You can face-guard once. Next time let the pass inbounds and trap, using the slides of the next section. Follow that with a safe "off." On the very next possession you could force a dribble and run a stunt to kill the dribble and steal the pass. By changing up like this you could use the jug all night, gaining steals and losing little to an attacking ball club.

Basic Slides of the Jug Press. Diagram 3-12 illustrates the basic slides of the jug press and its variation. Whether X1 lines up on the out-of-bounds passer or at the free throw line, he traps with the wing on the successful inbounded pass. X4 covers the vertical passing lane. X3 and X5, the two weakside defenders, have two different coverages available: one gambling and one safe. Because you chose the jug press, you are not worried about safety features. X3 would cover the horizontal passing lanes including 1 as he stepped inbounds. X5 denies any diagonal pass, and X4 blankets the vertical passing lane. As a variation or because of safety beliefs, X3 could deny the diagonal lane while shading the horizontal. X5 would drop to cover long passes and play free safety. X4 still occupies the vertical.

A pass to 4, representing the second trapping area, would employ the slides of Diagram 3-5 or Diagram 3-8, depending again on your conservatism. The third passing area, a pass from 4 to 5, would engage the Diagram 3-6 slides.

Alternating Slides of the 1-2-2 and 3-2 Presses. Diagram 3-13 is an alternate slide that offers an infinite series within itself. As the ball is entered to 2, X1 performs his customary trapping slide. X2 retreats, with his hands up, down the vertical lane until he encounters an offensive player. This prevents 2 from throwing a vertical pass and shows an open dribbling lane to 2. The tighter X1 plays 2, the more convinced 2 might become that a trap will ensue. X2 now has several options available. If 2 begins a dribble, X2 can jump toward 2. Then 2 might pick up his dribble. X1 would cover 2 tightly yelling "used." X2 retreats in the vertical lane. X4 leaves to play safety and to defend the long lob passes deep and over X5's head. X5 defends the diagonal lane and X3 hovers in the horizontal lane.

As 2 dribbles down the vertical lane, X2 could run-and-jump or run-and-trap with X1. On traps, X4 could return to the vertical lane, X5 to deep safety, and X3 to the diagonal; or on traps, X4 could stay at safety with X5 taking the vertical lane.

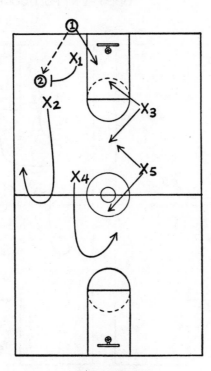

DIAGRAM 3-13

As 2 dribbles down the vertical lane, X1 could cut off his drive and work the give-the-outside—take-it-away with X3. X5 would shoot the horizontal gap while shading the diagonal. X4 could remain deep, or X4 could gap the diagonal lane for an interception. X2 would remain in the vertical lane.

While 2 rambles down the vertical lane, X3 would exercise his peel-back option. The slides again would require X5 to take the horizontal, X2 to remain in the vertical, and X4 to have the option of being safe or playing the diagonal.

All these options are available from the 1-2-2 or the 3-2. The same options are available with a different beginning slide. Diagram 3-14 shows X2 assuming the same duties as X1 did in Diagram 3-13. X1 slides into the vertical lane. X3, X4, and X5 still fill their same lanes.

Peel-Back. Diagram 3-15 depicts the peel-back from the odd zone fronts. With X1 playing on the ball while it is out-of-bounds and X5 playing safety, the line up could be the diamond press. X2 forces the dribble down the sideline. X1 sags well ahead of the dribbling 2. At the most opportune moment X1 slides into the vertical lane, denying further penetration by 2. X2 clamps the trap. X4, who originally dropped to

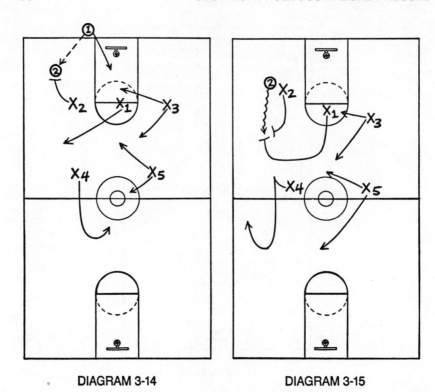

DIAGRAM 3-14   DIAGRAM 3-15

"show" 2 an open lane, covers the vertical lane. X3 and X5 can play it safe or they can gamble. X5 covers safety and X3 blankets the diagonal lane, shading the horizontal in safe play. When gambling becomes the order, X5 would deny the diagonal and X3 would hover just outside the horizontal.

Give-Outside—Take-It-Away. X2 encourages 2 to dribble down the vertical lane, and X4 "shows" 2 the lane is open (Diagram 3-16). At the most opportune moment, X2 turns 2 back to the middle. Just as 2 turns, X1 comes to trap. X1 might force 2 into a ball-handling error, or X1 might draw the charge if 2 continues. X3, who originally drops to protect the middle, shoots the horizontal gap to steal the "habit" pass. X5, who dropped deep, can come upcourt to cover the diagonal lane. X4 remains in the vertical lane.

Throwbacks. Diagram 3-12 represents the basic slides of the 1-2-2 zone press; we'll use it to discuss throwback passes. The short throwback to 1 would result in X3 and X1 trapping 1. X2 would drop to the middle to help on diagonal lane coverage but stay alert to a horizontal pass back to 2. X5 would cover the vertical passing lane to 3. X4 would drop to safety, or if you are aggressive, X4 would blanket the diagonal passing lane.

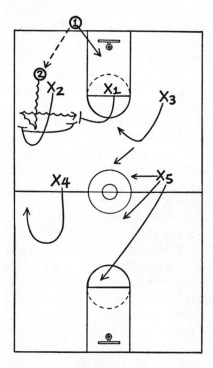

DIAGRAM 3-16

A long throwback pass from 2 to 3 (still using Diagram 3-12) would demand that X5 arrive as the ball arrives. X3 would come to the ball helping X5 trap 3. X5 first turns 3 outside, then he denies 3 that route (see chapter 1). Meanwhile, X1, X2, and X4 must recover while the pass is in the air and while X5 delays 3's next move. Two lane coverages are available: X4 gets the vertical lane, X2 covers the diagonal lane and the basket area, and X1 shades the horizontal lane while concentrating on helping X2 in the diagonal lane; or X4 can hurriedly retreat to the basket for safety purposes. Meanwhile, X2 races to cover the vertical lane and X1 helps X4 in the diagonal lane while being alert to the horizontal pass.

Combining Slides to Reduce Offensive Efficiency. You can combine the jug with the diamond, playing one after made free throws and the other after made baskets (for further strategies see chapter 10). While this would combine slides and reduce offensive efficiency, it means you do not teach a defense completely. You will not get as much out of your defenses because all coaches drill daily against the major presses. You could combine the jug or diamond with the box or one of its variations.

You could teach only the jug and teach it completely, alternating the slides as it becomes necessary to combat what your opponents wish to use against your press. This requires excellent bench coaching. For example, you open the game in Diagram 3-12 but play it safe. Your opponents discover the horizontal opening. You close it as shown in Diagram 3-13, possibly getting a few interceptions and an easy basket or two from "habit" passes.

Then 2 discovers the open vertical dribbling lane. He begins, and you close it with the peel-back (Diagram 3-15). Player 2 decides not to dribble, so you answer with Diagram 3-13, covering the passing lanes, playing it safe, and still pressuring 2. You make 2 narrow his choices. You make 2 nervous because of the ten-second count rule, maybe with "off" a time or two. Since 2 cannot pass because the lanes are covered, 2 knows a trap will answer his dribble. But you change to a run-and-jump the next few times. Player 2 dribbles; he is confused. To 2 the situation looks hopeless: it looks like 20 defenders are on the court. Your press works whether you steal a pass or not. You have their best ball handler working into your hands. You can even face-guard or deny. When they think they have solved your press, you can again answer with "off." Not only have you altered your slides to confuse your opponents, but you have changed the tempo of the game by changing the pace of your press.

Changing the Pace of Your Jug Press. If you want to press an entire game, you never want your opponent to get used to a slide or the tempo. These are your two best areas to change the solutions to your press. Just as you feel your opponents have adjusted to the slide you are using, change it. Change it to close off the area they are attacking. You have pre-drilled slides, numbered in a way your defenders will understand. Call that number.

Besides shortstopping, leftfielding, and slides, you can alter the pressure points. Don't trap the primary areas only. Trap the secondary areas. Never change just to change. Force the offense to make you change, but change just before they have succeeded. As you gain experience you will get a feel for when the change should occur.

The greatest way to change the pace of the press is to go from an "on" stunt to an "off." This is especially true in the jug press. The jug press emphasizes aggressive, all-out defensive maneuvers with five men in backcourt. "Off" pressures the ball but offers many changes. In "on" you fan; in "off" you funnel. In "on," you compel a pass or stunt off the dribble, gambling frequently for a turnover; in "off," you allow the attack to advance up the court, but they had better be careful.

When 1 passes into 2 and you are in "off" you can use the slides of Diagrams 3-12, 3-13, or 3-14. For discussion let's use the Diagram 3-12 slides. X2 covers 2 aggressively, trying to keep 2 thinking the press is "on." But X2 turns 2 inside. X1 drops to the middle lane above the ball, keeping passes out of the diagonal lane into the middle. X3 drops even deeper, denying any flash pivot move to the central diagonal lane. X4 denies any vertical pass. X5 defends the basket being ever alert to lob passes.

A pass completed over X2 or X1 has these two defenders racing to a point above the ball. The defender on the new receiver stays with the ball handler. The two front players do the adjusting. A pass completed on the left side has X1 and X4 up front while a pass completed on the right side shows X3 and X2 up front. These four continue in their zone defense until ball arrives safely to a predesignated point in the frontcourt.

"Off" tends to slow the tempo. But you can thoroughly confuse your opponents by face-guarding the inbounds pass, utilizing a left-fielder, shortstop, or centerfielder and immediately upon the successful entry of the ball going to "off." The next possession face-guard and go to a trap immediately upon successful entry.

Adjustments. Adjustments within the press can take two forms: You can change slides or you can change tempos. Both have been discussed already. This section offers another type of adjustment: Keeping the same formation but changing the basic objectives of the press.

There are many ways you can do this: By no means is this adjustment the only one. Most offenses attempt to hit an attacker breaking into the middle lane or posting there and then dishing the ball to a cutter breaking down the opposite outside lane; this adjustment nullifies this attack completely. This particular adjustment also is a complete continuous pressing defense within itself.

Diagrams 3-17 and 3-18 demonstrate the continuous movement on throwback passes. It is a super gambling defense. It gives the appearance of man-to-man coverage on the cutter in the outside lane.

Player 1 passes inbounds to 2 (Diagram 3-17). Player 2 wanted to hit a teammate in the middle lane who, in turn, will pass to teammate 3 breaking down the outside lane. Most high school teams use a variation of this full-court attack. X5 is to deny the ball to that attacker in the middle lane. Even if it is complete, the receiver in the middle lane would have to be careful on his pass or X3 would intercept it. When 2 receives the ball, X3 begins his floating to deep safety, timing his departure to coincide with any pass into the central lane. If no pass is made to the central lane, you could play X3 in the horizontal passing lane between 2 and 3. (You could send X3 deep regardless.)

Diagram 3-18 depicts the recovery system of slides on throwback passes. Player 2 passes to 3. X5 traps with X1 on 3. This opens a "habit" pass from 3 to the middle lane, but X4 hustles into perfect interception position. Even if X4 gets there late, he pressures the new receiver who has been taught to dish off to 2 cutting up the outside lane. That is difficult if not impossible because X2 is breaking down that lane. X3 comes back to blanket the vertical lane.

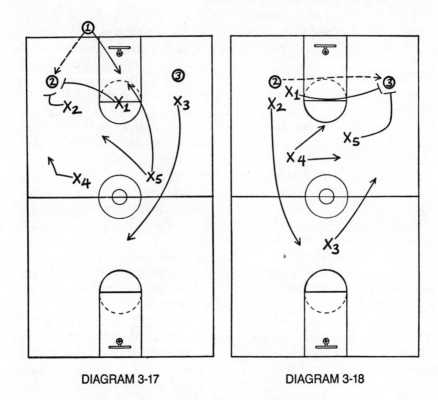

DIAGRAM 3-17   DIAGRAM 3-18

A pass back from 3 to 2 would require X4 to trap 2 with X1. X3 would deny passes into the middle lane, and X5 would race up the outside lane to deep positioning. X2 would return to vertical lane coverage. This defense continues with X2, X3, and X5 responsible for running the basic movements. X1 would be your weakside defender, your slowest player. He only has to trap. All the others not only have to trap, they have to deny passes, and they have to get quickly to distant passing lanes. The beauty of the adjustment is that all gap shooters are moving toward their interceptions; even if they don't intercept, you will still have a safety defender deep.

4

Hybrid Full-Court
Zone Presses

Hybrid zone presses will never achieve the popularity of the regular zone press alignments, except for the match-up. But there is a place for them in basketball. They are effective as a change-up, and they also force the offensive team to prepare specially for your defense. No team can effectively train for a press in only two or three pre-game practice sessions. Your hybrid defense has the advantage in preparations. Whenever you have the exact but unique personnel required for a particular hybrid, you have your perfect press for that year; and that press can lead your team to the ultimate championship.

THE MATCH-UP

Match-up zone presses can deny the inbounding of the ball; they can permit the pass inbounds but influence where it goes; or they can leave the entry to the discretion of the offense. Any zone press alignment can become your initial positioning. Each works equally well. The formation you choose should be based on your objectives and your personnel. The key to success is to place your key personnel where they can do their best.

You can begin zone and rule a zone after the entry pass. Or you can begin man-to-man, which offers considerable more pressure, and rule a zone after the ball is inbounded. You can even wait until after the second pass, the first pass after the ball has been inbounded, before trapping and going zone. This means you stay matched-up or man-to-man after the pass inbounds (the first pass). On the next pass, you trap and zone the passing lanes. If the ball is advanced by dribbling, you could have your defenders run and "jump" or run and "trap". Or the dribble could key two defenders to trap while two play the passing lanes and one covers the basket. Experienced clubs handle this strategy better than inexperienced ones.

Basically, then, there are two ways to play your match-up zone press: start man and rotate to a zone, or start zone and rotate to a zone. Both have merit, but both must never be taught to the same ball club: defensive confusion would result. One (the man-to-man beginning) offers more pressure; the other, however, provides more structure, less required reaction by the individual defenders.

Start Man and Rotate to a Zone. Because each defender begins coverage on a man, your club does not need match-up coverage rules. They already cover one attacker each. You can decide if you wish to deny or face-guard, shortstop or centerfield, or allow the pass inbounds. You can virtually force the pass where you want it.

Once the ball is inbounded, you play man-to-man, covering all cutters, until the ball is dribbled. When the inbound receiver begins his dribble, your defenders revert to zone coverage. To accomplish this umbrella effect of the passing lanes, you must have team rules.

Player 1 has inbounded the ball to 2 (Diagram 4-1). X2 pressures 2 hard, trying to get 2 to dribble. X1, X3, and X4 deny passes to their assigned men. Any pass should be deflected, stolen. A dribble by 2 usually results.

If 2 dribbles toward X1, X1 and X2 double-team 2. X3 and X4 gap the three receivers (there are usually three outlet areas in all zone press offenses). Diagram 4-2 shows this gapping. X5 comes as high as midcourt. Player 2 should not be able to find 5.

If 2 had dribbled toward X3 initially, X3 and X2 would have trapped. X4 and X1 would have gapped. X5 would still have coverage duties around the midcourt area.

All defenders must be taught how to trap and how to gap the attacking passing lanes (umbrella). No defender will know where his position will be on the entry pass because he began man-to-man. He will cover his man wherever he cuts before the pass is inbounded.

Unless you plan to teach a match-up zone press which has only one trapping area, you will need some rules to cover the second and the third traps. This makes your match-up a true zone press.

Passing lane defenders must keep the ball out of the middle of the court. A pass there defeats your press, but you should organize an orderly retreat. An example of the middle lane reception: 4 flashes to

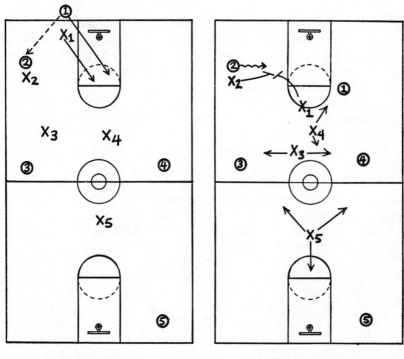

DIAGRAM 4-1   DIAGRAM 4-2

the middle lane in Diagram 4-1. Both X4 and X3 miss the coverage as 2 completes his pass to 4. The nearest defender, X3 or X4, covers 4 as he receives the pass. The other defender races deep to help X5 defend the basket area. X1 and X2 split 4, one breaking downcourt on the right side of 4 and the other streaking down the left side of 4. This movement prevents 4 from making an immediate dribble or pass.

Defenders want to force the pass around the perimeter. The rules are simple: The gap shooter on the side of the pass contains the new receiver, waiting for his teammate to come and help him trap. The gap shooter away from the pass should drop deep as a safety. The safety should become the vertical lane defender. Whichever one of the original trappers had the ball passed over his head or around him goes to help double-team the new receiver. The other trapper drops to cover the middle lane while shading the horizontal. These rules continue as the ball is advanced downcourt around the perimeter. Each time there is a successful pass, the ball is pushed to the outside and trapped.

In Diagram 4-2, a pass from 2 to 1 would result in X4 and X1 double-teaming 1. X5 would race to the vertical passing lane between 1 and 4. X3 would scamper to safety, near the midcourt line. X2 drops to cover the middle lane, the pass toward 3.

If 2 had passed to 3 originally (Diagram 4-2), the double-team would have been employed by X3 and X2. X5 would have covered the vertical passing lane, and X4 would have dropped to safety, this time near the free throw line. X1 would have charged into the diagonal passing lane, shading the horizontal.

Should X5 be an exceptional shot blocker, a defender you would want to keep at safety, you could alter your rules. Instead of having the weakside original gap shooter drop to deep safety, you simply require him to cover the vertical passing lane. This frees X5 to always be the safety.

To match-up zone press by starting in man-to-man defense allows you to pressure inbounds passes tighter. It also exerts maximum pressure once the ball has entered the playing surface. But it requires your players to be able to read passing lanes and to move intelligently as a unit. It requires more basketball savvy.

Frequently you can trap the inbounds pass before the dribble. This reduces the offensive clearouts. It keeps the offense guessing; and more important to the defense, it keeps several offensive players in backcourt.

Sometimes, however, in order to get open to receive the inbounds pass, especially when denial defense is being played, the movement of the offense can distort your zone press coverage. This can occur only when both wing men, X2 and X3, cover cutters to the ball on the same side of the floor (Diagram 4-3). Rules for each defender would place proper responsibilities and reduce alibis. X2 had initial left-lane duties; X3 had right lane responsibilities. These do not change: the wing man opposite the ball entry plays that passing lane—the horizontal. Because the ball entered to 4, X2 must race to cover the opposite passing lane, the horizontal (Diagram 4-3). If 2 had received the inbounds pass, then X3 would have covered the horizontal lane. That was X3's original lane, so the duty passed on to him.

Rule: When the ball is entered away from X3 but into his original assigned lane, he (X3) must race to deep safety coverage (Diagram 4-3). X4 would trap with X1. X2 has the horizontal lane, and X5 covers the vertical lane. X3 would cover deep. A summary of these passing lane rules follows:

a. Wing man opposite ball entry lane plays that lane and shades the diagonal;

b. Wing man opposite ball side, but where ball entered his original assigned position, races to deep coverage;

c. X4 or X5 always covers the vertical passing lane if not involved in the trap;

d. If X4 or X5 has his vertical lane covered, the other one plays deep safety;

e. X1 always traps horizontally on the inbounds pass.

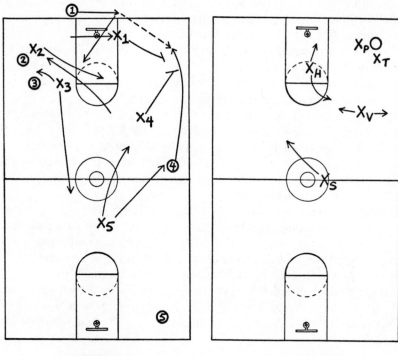

DIAGRAM 4-3   DIAGRAM 4-4

The passing lanes rules will always create an umbrella and two men on the ball trapping; this allows an instinctive coverage on all throwbacks for a secondary trap coverage (Diagram 4-4).

Xp, the point defender, traps with Xt, who will be X4, X3, or X2. Xh, the horizontal passing lane defender, will be X3 or X2. Xv, the vertical passing lane defender, will always be X4 or X5. Xs, the safety, will be X2, X3, X4, or X5. A short throwback, a pass in front of Xh, would find Xh and Xp trapping, Xt denying the horizontal lane, Xs defending the vertical, and Xv dropping to deep safety. Another way to say it is that the deep defender covers vertical, vertical covers deep, trapper covers horizontal, horizontal and point traps.

A deep throwback has Xs and Xh trapping. Xv defends the vertical, Xt plays safety, and Xp races to the horizontal passing lane (Diagram 4-4).

A successful pass in front of the vertical defender ends with Xv and Xt trapping. Xs defends the vertical passing lane, Xh covers the basket playing safety, and Xp hovers in the horizontal passing lane.

Start Zone and Stay in a Zone. A match-up zone implies one-on-one coverage. To start in a zone, you need a man on the out-of-bounds passer. Your zone press therefore must begin 1-2-1-1 or 1-2-2 or some form of the odd zone front. You could drop the defender on the ball to a centerfield position, but he must quickly return to his original duties (X1 in Diagram 4-5). However, this adjustment allows your zone to appear as an even front. Because of space and because the 1-2-1-1 offers the best match-up positioning we will use only the diamond formation to show the match-up zone press from an original zone alignment.

Rules are a must if you intend to "match" the offense's original alignment. X2 takes the first attacker on the left of X1. X3 has the player on X1's right. If you wish to deny ball entry, X1, X2, X3, and X4 use the techniques described in chapter 3 in the diamond press sections. X4 takes the third attacker downcourt and X5 blankets the fourth attacker downcourt. This makes your zone formation evolve into the same pattern as the offensive alignment.

X1 plays the out-of-bounds passer as tightly as possible without going over the endline. He shades the inside of the court trying to force a pass to the corners. When the pass does reach an inbounds attacker, X1 drops toward the middle of the court even with the line of the ball. He plays this position until the ball moves. If the ball is dribbled toward X1, he traps. If the ball is dribbled or passed vertically by the wing defender, X1 drops hurriedly to cover the diagonal passing lane, shading the horizontal. If the pass is originally thrown back to the man who inbounds

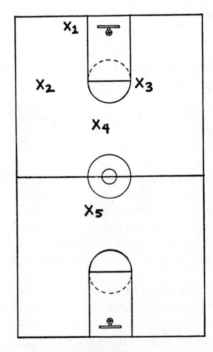

DIAGRAM 4-5

the ball as he steps inbounds, X1 tries to force the ball out of the middle. If the ball is passed across the free throw line, X1 sinks to the new line of the ball, still covering the middle. A ball passed or dribbled into the middle lane mandates a quick retreat to the basket area for half-court defense.

X2 and X3 have the same duties. When the ball is on their side of the court, they are the strong side wings. When the ball is on the opposite side, they are called weakside wings.

Strongside wing, when in denial or face-guard, matches the attacker on his side. With the ball out-of-bounds, both X2 and X3 are considered strongside wings. If no one is in their area, they drop immediately toward the half-court line and to the middle until they get eye contact with an attacker. They play between their man and the ball, when denying, even if it means being blind to the ball. If the ball is successfully thrown in front of them, they pressure tightly, hoping to demand a dribble. Sometimes the strongside wing might try to force the dribble outside then take it away. If the dribble starts toward the middle, X1 traps with the strongside wing. If the dribble goes outside, the strongside wing traps with the short-safety, X4. If the dribbler gets by these trappers, the strongside wing follows behind the dribbler, trying to flick the dribble away. If the ball is passed vertically, the strongside wing traps with the short-safety. If it is passed horizontally, the strongside wing becomes the weakside wing. If the ball is passed deep or sharply to the middle, the strongside wing retreats to the half-court defense.

Weakside wing plays as a strongside wing until the ball is passed inbounds. When the ball is inbounded away from your side, the weakside wing drops at a 45-degree angle to take away any diagonal pass. Any cutter into this area must be denied the pass. A pass into the middle kills the press. The weakside wing can pass cutters to the short-safety (breaking too far to the strong side) or to X1 (breaking too far to the horizontal lane). If the ball is passed to the middle area, intercept it or deflect it. If it is completed, pressure the receiver, forcing a few moments delay while your teammates retreat. If the pass is completed vertically or dribbled there, the weakside wing retreats to the basket area and becomes the new safety unless the safety has been told to stay at home. If the safety, X5, stays home, the weakside wing must cover the new vertical passing lane. If the pass out of the first trap was horizontal, the weakside wing now becomes the new strongside wing and the press continues.

The short-safety, X4 in Diagram 4-5, must be your best athlete. He initially reads the offensive attack, picks up the third cutter to the ball when face-guarding, and helps on lob passes over the wing's head. Once the ball comes inbounds, X4 lines up behind the strongside wing, playing the vertical passing lane but shading the diagonal. He accepts cutters from the weakside wing. He must stay in constant communication with his wings. If the ball is dribbled up the sideline past the wing but in front of the short-safety, X4 traps with the strongside wing. When the ball is passed horizontally across the free throw lane out of the first trap, the short-safety becomes the safety and the safety becomes the short-safety. If the ball is passed deep, the short-safety hustles to help the safety until help can arrive. On any successful pass to the middle of the court, X4 retreats to the top of the circle and plays a tandem defense with X5.

X5, the safety, matches the man farthest from the ball after it has been inbounded. He should come forward to near midcourt on good traps. If the pass goes horizontally across the free throw lane, X5 takes the new vertical passing lane. If the ball is dribbled down the sideline by the wing or passed to a spot in front of X4, X5 takes the new vertical passing lane—but only after he sees the weakside wing can cover the basket area for him. This man must have good judgment. He must know how to play a two-on-one and a three-on-one breakaway situation. He must accept and love a challenge. If he is a shot blocker and you want him to stay home at safety, then X4, the short-safety, must always cover the vertical lane, or trap while the weakside wing has the vertical lane. X5 must know who the opponent's shooters are. He may have to leave the basket area to stop a shooter; but even when he does this, he should be sure the short-safety or the wing from the weak side will have the basket area covered. On any long pass, X5 must use excellent delaying tactics until help arrives. While X4 must be your best athlete, X5 must have the best judgment.

THE MINOR ZONE PRESSES

While the basic slides of the diamond and the box presses have shown their merit over the years, there appears almost every year a zone press that is different, that intrigues the basketball purist's mind, that works so wonderfully well. This press has success for a year or two and other coaches begin to copy it. But they never reach the original plateau enjoyed by the creator of the unique press. So the coaches go back to the standard, disillusioned. Many reasons are advanced for their failure: poor teaching, not executed correctly, the offense caught up with it, etc. But the fact remains, the hybrid press was once ultrasuccessful. Even its originator discards it after a few years of failure.

There is a press for every type of personnel. The hybrid press will work as long as it has the correct chemistry and the proper personnel. All presses, except the man-to-man, have such weaknesses. They can be exploited. With the right personnel, those weaknesses are less evident, the press less vulnerable.

This section presents four presses that will work with the right players: the Y, the 2-1-1 and monster, the 1-1-1-1-1, and the two plus a triangle. You may create the next perfect press for your unique personnel that will lead others to try to emulate you. Ultimately they will fail because they do not have that special blend. Your opponents, while facing that perfect union of talent and slides, may be in for some long, long nights.

There are three ways you can play your hybrid press. With the perfect personnel, it could be your only press. With perfect or near-perfect personnel, it could be your change-up press, your complementary press. Even with less perfect personnel, it could be an off-beat "trick" defense run only a few possessions each half, designed to create a turnover or confusion or to take a team out of its patterned offense.

Because these presses are unique, practice time must be spent specifically preparing for them. This gives your press the advantage in preparations before the game even begins.

Y Press. Three-point guards and two lean, tall, quick, agile forwards make the best crew for your 2-1-1-1 (Y) zone press. X1 and X2 would be your agile forwards (Diagram 4-6). They need average quickness and adequate size. X3, X4, and X5 need to be quick, speedy, darting players, like most point guards. If they happen to have size, that is another plus. Savvy and aggressiveness are more important.

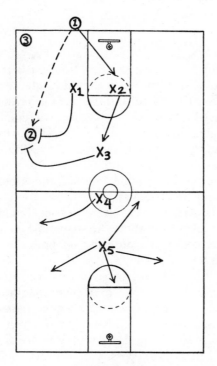

DIAGRAM 4-6

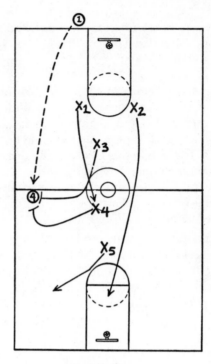

DIAGRAM 4-7

X1 and X2 can face-guard the first two attackers downcourt. X3 helps on the lob pass. X3 also covers the third attacker downcourt. X4 would pick up the fourth attacker if the offense is having trouble getting the ball inbounds. A lob inbounds pass to either sideline in backcourt would result in X3 gambling for the deflection. Failing to get a deflection would find X3 trapping with the forward (X1 or X2) on the entry side. Diagram 4-6 shows a lob pass to 2 at the 28-foot marker. X4 is already in position to cover the vertical passing lane. X2, the opposite wing, covers the diagonal lane and X5 covers safety.

A pass thrown nearer to midcourt or deeper should be deflected by X4. A pass further downcourt allows X5 to gamble for the steal and for X4 to retreat to the basket. Because the sidelines appear open, many teams will try these longer passes.

A pass made inbounds in front of X1 or X2 could be covered in either of two ways. X1 could force 3 to dribble (Diagram 4-6). X3 would then trap with X1 as X4 and X2 cover their regular passing lanes. Or you could have X1 and X2 trap. X3 would deny passes down the vertical lane and X4 would occupy the diagonal, shading the horizontal.

On any short throwback pass, X2 recovers to handle the new receiver. X3, X4, and X5 recover to their normal positions. If you prefer

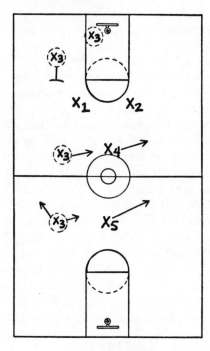

DIAGRAM 4-8

more pressure, X5 could rotate to become the new trapper with X2. Then X4 rotates to the new vertical lane and X3 becomes the deep safety. This type of mad scramble can sometimes put a defender into an intended passing lane.

Because the sidelines look open, deeper passes result more often than not. In Diagram 4-7, X4 would hurry to 4, deflecting the pass if possible. If X4 arrives late, he must detain 4. X3 comes hard to trap with X4. X2 races to deep safety. X1 gets as high as the ball, playing the horizontal and shading the diagonal passing lanes. X5 covers the vertical passing lane as soon as he sees X2 can recover to the basket.

Because of the quickness of these five defenders, they can constantly gamble. They can make up any loss of rebounding power by accumulating steals. The 2-1-1-1 is an excellent complementary defense to the man-to-man press.

The 2-1-1 Plus a Monster. This defense serves two purposes: as a complete defense by itself, or as a defense working in conjunction with the 2-1-1-1. You need virtually the same type material as you needed for the Y zone press: two lean, agile, quick forwards (X1 and X2) and two point-guard types (X4 and X5). X3, the monster, needs to be ultra-aggressive, have excellent savvy, and be the best defensive player in your league (Diagram 4-8).

Where you put X3 calls the intentions of your press (Diagram 4-8). If you place X3 on the out-of-bounds passer, you intend to run the 1-2-1-1 zone press. If you put X3 on a particular attacker, usually an expert ball handler, one your opposition's offense depends heavily upon, you propose to run your box and a chaser (see Diagram 4-9) or you plan to trap receptions inbounds after face-guarding by running your 1-2-1-1. If you put X3 near midcourt, he moves X4 out of the middle and you will run the slides of the 2-2-1. If you drop X3 deeper near X5 you either run a 2-1-2 or you run three men chasing (X1, X2, and X4) and two men tandem (X3 and X5). All these defenses have been presented earlier except the three men and a tandem and the box and a chaser.

The three men and a tandem is used against teams who attack well against normal full-court pressure. They also attack the basket when they break the press. It is the simplest of all defenses. Two of the three defenders (X1, X2, and X4) trap the ball while one shades a passing lane (see chapter 1 for gap shooting techniques). Any interception gained is a plus. Any completion has this gap shooter trapping with his other closest

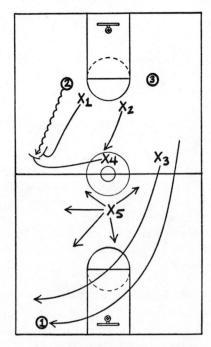

DIAGRAM 4-9

teammate and the lone defender becomes the new gap shooter. These three continue this strategy until the ball crosses half-court. X3 and X5 gap any deep defenders. Should X3 and X5 face an attack by the ball and some offensive players, they play tandem for a pass or two until help arrives. It is difficult to get a layup or a short jumper against this defense, and it keeps pressure on the offense. Often patterned teams, which experience a high degree of success against regular zone pressure, have trouble adjusting to the three men and a tandem.

Diagram 4-9 shows the box and a chaser. X1 and X2 set up between midcourt and the free throw line. X4 begins around the circle at midcourt. X5 plays about the 28-foot marker on the defensive end. X3 chases the opponent's best ball handler. There are many teams who are lost without their adept passer-dribbler controlling their offense. More and more defensive teams have started chasing this player instead of the opponent's leading scorer.

As long as the ball stays in front of X1 or X2, the defender covering the ball, X1 in Diagram 4-9, pressures tightly. The other front defender, X2, drops to the middle lane coverage. Remember the ball is in the hands of the second-best ball handler, at best. X4 shades toward the vertical passing lane. When 2 dribbles or passes the ball forward, X1 and X4 trap. X5 covers the vertical lane and gaps the diagonal lane. X2 covers the diagonal and shades the horizontal. If the ball were passed to 3, X2 would cover 3 and X1 would sink to middle lane coverage. X5 would become the new vertical lane interceptor and X4 would drop deep. Any successful pass into the middle lane breaks the press.

Another variation for the 2-1-1 and a monster: Instead of defending against the top ball handler, have the monster play in the lane of your opponent's primary attack. This requires you as the coach to decide how your opponents are trying to break your press; for example—pass to the middle lane and dish the ball out. Because your monster always stays in the diagonal lane, your opponents must abandon their primary plans or face interception after interception. As soon as they show their secondary attack plans, reassign the monster man. This is bench coaching with a 2-1-1 and a monster.

The 1-1-1-1-1. Passive presses need not be created. "Off" from any regular zone press or man-to-man results in a passive defensive scheme. Hybrid pressure must, by nature, be active. One of the most dynamic and most aggressive is the 1-1-1-1-1. Small, quick, lively players run this best, but it has worked for teams that get progressively taller and slower. You still need at least three very aggressive defenders. They should occupy X2, X3, and X4 in Diagram 4-10. Your tallest or slowest defender could handle either X1 or X5.

X1 can start on the out-of-bounds passer with X2, X3, X4, and X5 staggered about ten or fifteen feet behind him. This is best when X1 is slow or when you are sure your opponents will throw inbounds in front of X3. If your opponents prefer to throw to midcourt or further, X1 should line up at the free throw line with X2, X3, X4, and X5 still staggered ten to fifteen feet in progression. The defenders still line up even with the ball.

Down the middle, where most zone presses attack, defensive strength of the 1-1-1-1-1 is obvious. This formation and the fear of passing long usually focus entry to one side of the court. Once the ball is entered, the defense attacks. The defense wants to keep the ball going down the sidelines.

Diagram 4-10 exhibits the defensive movement on a short thrown in. X2 and X1 immediately attack 2. X3 darts to close off the horizontal and to shade the diagonal. X4 hovers in the vertical, being aware of movement in the diagonal. X5 plays safety, but also covers the diagonal. Notice the defenders are all on the move toward the pass, making interception much easier.

Diagram 4-11 displays a longer pass, a difficult crosscourt pass. An active X3 or X4 might deflect or intercept this maneuver, but if the interception fails they should trap. As the pass flies, X2 races to deep diagonal. When X5 sees this he covers the vertical. X1 hustles to deny any horizontal pass.

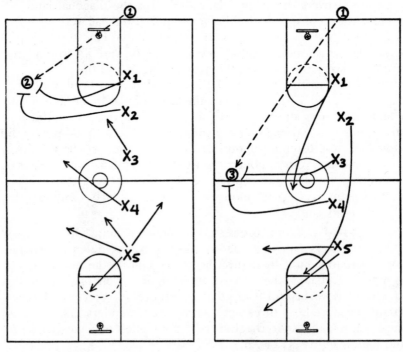

DIAGRAM 4-10   DIAGRAM 4-11

X1, X2, X3, and X4 in that order could play denial or face-guard.

Secondary trapping areas can be plotted by combining Diagram 4-11 with any of the sequence of diagrams in chapter 3. A proper sequence could be Diagrams 3-4, 3-5, 4-11, 3-6, and 3-9. Another possibility would be Diagrams 3-7, 3-8, 4-11, and 3-9. Certainly this press begins differently and can destroy offensive teams who believe solely in getting the ball to the middle lane. It can be used as a mad scrambling press by giving your players a great deal of freedom as to when to attack, when and where to trap, and options as far as coverage of passing lanes. It can be kept even safer than diagramed by allowing only one player to cover the initial inbounds pass. Then you would trap at the first hint of a dribble. Judge your personnel and create, create, create.

Two Plus Triangle. The two plus triangle is a one-spot press. It cannot be regrouped for a secondary trapping area because of the personnel involved. You have three quick players and two very slow ones. The two slow ones must be tall, center types. The three quick defenders can be point-guard types or wing types.

This press can be altered as to where you set it up. You can "trap" the out-of-bounds passer. Or you can force an inbounds receiver to commence a dribble, then kill the dribble and activate your press. In fact, an excellent place to trap an out-of-bounds passer is after a violation has occurred. The passer cannot move without walking.

Diagram 4-12 shows X1 (one of your tall, slow defenders) showing the outside to 1, taking it away, and X2 (your other tall, slow defender) killing 1's dribble. X3, X4, and X5, your quick, agile defenders, form their triangle and gamble for the interception. Because X1 and X2 are tall, 1 will have trouble throwing over or around active hands and feet. X3, X4, and X5 are quick and smart; they will pick off lots of passes. Because of the three quick players and because 1 would have to throw high on a long lob pass, very few layups will result. It is a safe press, but it produces only one primary trapping area.

When 2 passes into 1, X1 covers him tightly, trying to force 1 to dribble outside (Diagram 4-12). X1 keeps a cushion if he intends to cut 1's dribble off. X2 could cut the dribble off with a peel-back defensive maneuver, but here we use the give-the-outside—take-it-away stunt for explanation purposes. X1 and X2 will trap regardless of the maneuver used. To form the triangle, X3 lines up in the vertical lane (X4 if entered on the other side), denying a pass to any receiver there. X4 covers any flash pivot to the middle. X5 forms the apex of the triangle by placing himself directly between X3 and X4. Once the trap is set, X3, X4, and X5 must be given complete freedom to cover the lanes. They will get more than they will give. Even if one of them misses, the other two because of their quickness can prevent any successful attack near their defensive basket.

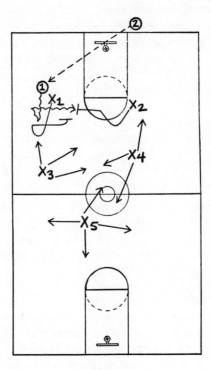

DIAGRAM 4-12

Rebound Zone Press. The odd (chapter 3) and the even (chapter 2) zone presses are here to stay. They have proven their worth. The match-up zone press is solid and gaining popularity every year. It will become a defensive staple. Hybrids will spring up annually and be successful before they begin to fail. Basketball will be all the better for each.

Then there are those nights when you cannot press because you cannot score from your set offenses or fast breaks. You need to press because you are behind. Enter the rebound press.

Almost all offensive teams send three and one-half players to the offensive boards and keep one and one-half back for defense. This is the formation from which the rebound press begins (Diagram 4-13). For maximum execution X3, X4, and X5 need to be quick and agile offensive rebounders. X2 needs good quickness and X1 needs to have the best speed.

The two rebounders on the side of the defensive rebound trap (Diagram 4-14). X3 and X4 trap because the rebound caromed off near them. The other rebounder, X5, has the horizontal passing lane duties. The short-safety, X2, covers the vertical or outlet pass lane. The deep safety, X1, prevents any deep pass, yet also gambles for a poorly thrown diagonal pass.

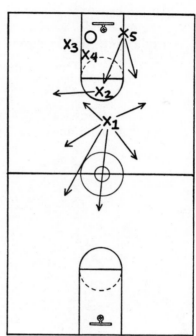

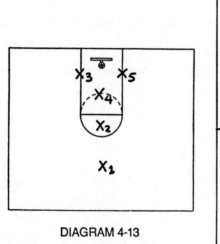

DIAGRAM 4-13

DIAGRAM 4-14

Instead of placing X2 at the free throw line and X1 deep, you could place them side by side, like in a 1-2-2 zone press, near the 28-foot marker. Under this condition, both X1 and X2 should possess good speed. The guard on the side of the rebound covers the outlet pass area, the vertical passing lane, and the other guard plays safety but shades the diagonal passing lane.

You can run the same trap and umbrella coverage on throwback passes that you used on all the other zone presses. Your rebound press defense does not have to be a one-trap defense.

The rebound press has many advantages:

a. It enables a team to press the opponent's poorest ball handlers.

b. A team can press even when they cannot score.

c. It is simple to teach and easy to apply.

d. It teaches aggressive offensive rebounding and aggressive constant defense.

e. It provides great pressuring possibilities against the well-disciplined or patterned ball clubs.

f. It teaches instant conversion from offense to defense.

g. It can be taught during defensive rebounding drills and can use the same slides as the zone press you already use, requiring very little additional practice time.

h. It is a most effective means of stopping the opponent's fast break.

i. It can force a deliberate team into a faster, upbeat tempo.

j. It teaches constant alertness, an ingredient easily recognizable in all championship teams.

5

Drop-Back Presses

Drop-back zone presses differ extensively from the full-court zone presses and the half-court traps. They are easily distinguishable because of their placement of personnel: Full-court presses deploy three or four defenders in the backcourt while the half-court traps place three or four defenders on or near the midcourt line. Drop-back presses, in essence, represent the area between the full-court presses and the half-court traps.

Because of this deployment, neither the full-court press offenses nor the half-court trap attacks are effective against the drop-back. A different offensive thrust must be mustered or the defense will gain the upper hand. A team that has not practiced against drop-back presses cannot be very successful for long against them.

Drop-back zone presses are gaining in popularity as a change-up defense. They encourage the offense to throw over the head of the midcourt defenders. These "lob" passes are easy prey for the back-line defenders who drill against them daily in practice. They can frequently use the same slides as their regular full-court zone press or even their half-court basket protecting zone, leaving little or nothing new to teach defensively. But they require much work offensively if the offense is to produce continuously. Drop-back zone presses usually use only one trapping area and at best two. Because of these characteristics the drop-back zone press could be considered a "trick" defense instead of a solid one. Included in their "tricks," however, are many solid stunts.

Athletes who cannot execute full-court presses because of skill limitations can successfully destroy offensive attacks with the drop-back presses. Drop-back defenders do not have to possess as much quickness or speed or savvy as their court-covering counterparts. Where the half-court traps are continuous defenses, requiring some foot quickness, the drop-back press is a one-attempt-steal "stunt" and then back into a solid half-court basket protecting defense. Because of this characteristic, slow players, who zone defensively near their basket, can gamble with the drop-back press. Quick players who also have good jumping skills can devour opponents in a matter of moments.

All drop-back presses must keep the ball out of the middle of the court. They will allow crosscourt passes, remaining patient until the ball is advanced to the critical pressure points. The defenders play the ball as a team, each sliding while the pass is in the air or the ball is being dribbled. Once the trap or stunt is set, all defenders get to their obvious passing lanes immediately. This eliminates the direct pass, compelling the "lob" or "bounce," exactly what the defense has been waiting for. These passing-lane defenders stay mentally close to the man in their lane but physically they try to show an open passing lane. Once a pass is directed toward their man they step in for the interception.

Many stunts complement the basic defensive attack of the drop-back press. A backcourt defender, for example, can lane a pass to the crosscourt receiver, or he can apply pressure on the dribbler. He can recover, even if beaten to the pressure spot. A frontcourt defender can fake a trap—hedge—and maybe impel the dribbler to kill his dribble. Once the dribble is killed, "used" is yelled and each passing lane defender keeps his man from receiving a pass. The defender on the ball helps by harassing the ball handler, preventing him from finding an open receiver. If this killed dribble occurs in frontcourt, five seconds of denial coverage grants a turnover. If it occurs in backcourt, whatever remains of the ten-second count will get your team a turnover. Add to this the pressure presented by the midcourt line—teams must get over it in ten seconds but once over it they cannot pass back into backcourt—and you can easily see why the press is so effective.

Run-and-jump stunts also aid the basic defense, and they can be coupled, by experienced clubs, with the man-to-man press as well as the zone press. You can retreat from the run-and-jump into almost any half-court defense you want. All these defensive maneuvers are discussed in this chapter.

When coaches work against full-court pressure and half-court traps but neglect to prepare for the drop-back press, their clubs will suffer any time they face this unusual press. Offensive coaches train their players to stop before crossing midcourt, study the defense, and pass to an open man or dribble through the press. They train their attackers to beware of the trap just as they cross the half-court line. The half-court line and the sideline act as two extra defensive players, giving the defense five against seven.

By properly defensing the passing lanes, once the trap has been set, the drop-back press eliminates the direct pass to an open attacker and freedom. Any dribbler who crosses midcourt gets clamped just as he crosses the time-line. Unpoised ball handlers will "see" a lob, and this lob is just what the defense wants, just what they have drilled against and drilled against and drilled against in practice.

All dribblers who advance to the perimeter of the defense must be pressured, trapped, or stunted. All passes completed around the perimeter pressure spots must be trapped, stopped, pressured.

To be effective, hustle is a must. The front defenders must force the ball handler into position for the trap. Stunts help by confusing the ball handler, leaving him perplexed as to the defense's intentions. Off-the-ball defenders must quickly scamper to their assignments. Drop-back presses impose a frightful initial problem for the offense, but they do so only if every defender is in position to play his role in creating the pressure.

EVEN FRONT DROP-BACK PRESSES

Even front drop-back presses, the 2-2-1 and the 2-1-2, will never achieve the popularity that the odd front, the 1-2-2, the 1-3-1 and the 1-2-1-1, will enjoy. Even front drop-back presses simply lack the versatility of the odd front.

The 2-2-1 Drop-Back Press. Diagram 5-1 shows the initial alignment, and this diagram will enable us to discuss all possible coverages. X1 and X2 need to be adequately quick with long arms. X3 and X4 need to understand trapping techniques; the taller they are the better. X5 must be your quickest player and your best interceptor.

X1 and X2 could begin their coverage all the way downcourt, even defending the inbounds passer and/or the inbounds receiver. This might disguise the drop-back press. The attackers might think it is a full-court zone press. X1 and X2 could even force the ball to the middle and run-and-jump. But this must occur in deep backcourt. As the ball approaches midcourt, the defenders must make every effort to keep the ball out of the middle.

Player 1 dribbles the ball near midcourt with X1 pressuring (Diagram 5-1). If 1 slows, X1 uses dogging tactics. Player 1 would like to pause to consider his dilemma; X1 wants to move 1 immediately by pass or by dribble. X2 drops to protect the middle. X4 denies any flash into the middle. X3 denies 3 the ball by a direct pass. X5 waits, anxiously anticipating 1's "seeing" the lob.

A crosscourt pass to 2 finds X2 going out to pressure 2, X1 dropping to the middle, X4 denying the vertical pass, and X3 refusing to allow a flash pivot to the middle. X5 still awaits the lob.

If 1 makes the mistake of killing his dribble, X1 savagely attacks 1, hands waving in all directions, yelling "used," disconcerting 1 in every possible way. X2 denies 2 a pass, X3 prevents 3 the ball, X4 covers 5, and X5 chases 4. If 1 is in the backcourt and if 1 has waited six seconds before he killed his dribble, in four seconds the defense will have created a turnover. If 1 has crossed the time-line, in five seconds the defense will be awarded the ball.

Should 1 pass to 3 or dribble the ball into frontcourt, X1 and X3 trap. X5 covers the vertical passing lane, X4 shades the diagonal but really protects the basket, and X2 denies the horizontal pass.

A "lob" from 1 to 5 or from 1 to 4 should result in a steal or at least a deflection by X5. Any crosscourt completion has X2 and X1 exchanging duties and X3 and X4 doing likewise.

Secondary traps can be practiced to cover passes into the corner. But they are more dangerous to the defense, and they require a little better defensive personnel. A pass from 3 to 4, for example, would result in X5 and X3 trapping. X4 would defend the low post, X2 the weakside rebounding area, and X1 would cover the high post. A gambling interception passing lane coverage, called late in the game when you are behind, would have X2 covering the high post and X1 covering the passing lane back out to 3. X4 would still cover the low post with X5 and X3 trapping.

The 2-1-2 Drop-Back Press. Diagram 5-2 illustrates the other even drop-back zone press, the 2-1-2. In this press X3 must be your best athlete and defender. X4 and X5 should be good jumpers and good anticipators. Quickness is a secondary attribute.

X1 pressures 1, impelling 1 outside. X2 drops to protect the middle. X3 also offers help in the middle but anticipates stopping 1's dribble drive quickly or getting to 3 as 3 receives a pass. X4 shades over to the vertical lane while X5 drops toward safety but remains ready to steal the "lob" to 5.

If 1 dribbles across midcourt or passes to 3, X3 and X1 trap. X4 is already in the vertical passing lane. X5 has the basket area but shades the diagonal lane. X2 is already in the horizontal lane. A successful pass out of the trap results in all defenders dropping to their pre-called basket protecting defense.

Crosscourt passes require X2 and X1 to exchange duties and X4 and X5 to trade responsibilities.

Another trapping possibility does exist. A pass from 3 to 4 could have X4 and X3 trapping, X5 playing low post, X2 defending the weakside wing, and X1 hovering around high post. An unsafe gambling

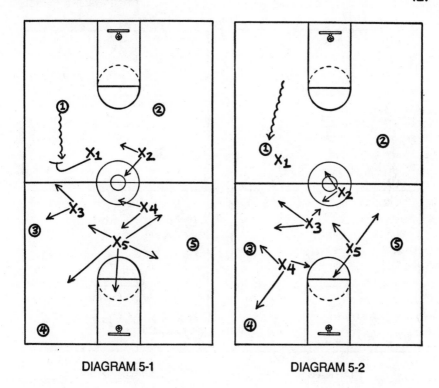

DIAGRAM 5-1   DIAGRAM 5-2

interception stunt, used late when behind, could allow X2 to cover high post and X1 to play the passing lane back out to 3.

ODD FRONT DROP-BACK PRESSES

Odd front drop-back presses offer more protection of the basket area, yet they generate greater pressure. They are also more flexible for developing stunts.

The 1-3-1 Drop-Back Press. The center circle area, covered by X5 in Diagram 5-3, remains the critical region for all drop-back presses. Passes completed there defeat your press. Fortunately the 1-3-1 drop-back press is strongest there. If X5 cannot handle this chore alone, X1 could drop into the jump circle and help.

As 1 approaches the critical perimeter areas, X4 begins to slide toward the vertical lane coverage, the same slide he would use in a regular 1-3-1 basket protecting zone defense. X3 drops toward deep safety (Diagram 5-3). If 1 continued his dribble toward the midcourt line, X1 and X2 would trap. X5 would have the horizontal lane, X4 the vertical, and X3 the diagonal and deep lanes.

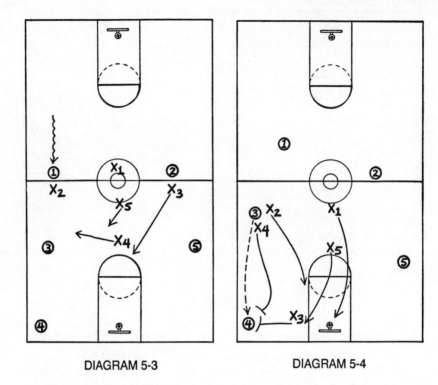

DIAGRAM 5-3   DIAGRAM 5-4

A pass from 1 to 2 would result in X3 hurrying back to his initial position and X4 racing cross the court and X2 dropping as X3 did originally.

If X2 has kept his body between 1 and 3, a "lob" pass would be required. X4 should easily intercept or deflect this pass. A lob from 1 to 4 would be even more up for grabs. A completed pass to either 3 or 4 offers a secondary trapping area, a trap you may or may not wish to teach. It depends on the speed and quickness of your personnel. In either case, X2 and X4 trap. X3 covers the basket lane but shades the vertical when 3 has the ball. He plays low post when 4 has the ball, but he also protects the basket. X5 has weak side if 4 receives the pass from 1. X1 plays the horizontal passing lane when 3 has the ball, and he defends the high post when 4 receives the pass from 1.

A crosscourt pass from 1 to 5 should be deflected by X3. If this crosscourt pass were successful, trapping could not effectively occur. X3 should delay 5 while X4, X5, and X2 retreat to the basket area. These three should reach protection positioning while the "lob" flies through the air. X1, meanwhile, retreats to his half-court defensive positioning.

There is a third potential trapping area: the pass from 3 to 4. Diagram 5-4 exhibits the coverage on the pass from 1 to 3 (see Diagram 5-3). X3 and X4 would trap the pass to 4. X5 would deny any pass into the low post. X1 has the weakside rebound and X2 covers the high post. The unsafe gambling optional coverage of the passing lanes is also available: X5 covers the low post; X1 shades the high post; and X2 refuses to allow a pass back out to 3.

To run the 1-3-1 press most effectively, a club needs above average height at X2 and X3 and above average quickness at X4. It helps if X2 and X3 anticipate well and can jump. Unless you plan stunts (see last section in this chapter), X1 and X5 can be ordinary or less defenders.

The 1-2-1-1 Drop-Back Press. The 1-2-1-1 drop-back press is the safest of all the odd drop-back zone presses. The 1-3-1 is the least safe, and the 1-2-2 splits the middle.

For the 1-2-1-1 drop-back press to work properly, a tall and excellent shot blocker must occupy the X5 position (Diagram 5-5). X2, X3, and X4 must be quick and fast, X4 being the quickest and the fastest. It helps if X1 has long arms. X1 can be your weakest defender unless you wish to stunt.

Most teams attack the 1-2-1-1 with a formation much like the one shown in Diagram 5-5, thinking the middle lane, the area around the jump circle, open. X4 must deny the pass to the middle until X3 can prevent it. X4 then hurries into the passing lane from 1 to 3.

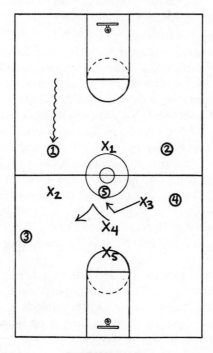

DIAGRAM 5-5

X1 plays a most important role. X1 can drop to help on the pass inside to 5, if that pass consistently gives the defense trouble. But X1's primary objective is to stay in the lane between 1 and 2. Occasionally he can deflect this pass from 1 to 2, but his lane positioning with his arms raised requires a "lob" pass, a very slow pass, one easily stolen. This also gives X3 and X4 time to recover, which they need to race to the weakside original coverage.

If the dribbling 1 approaches the time-line, X2 and X1 trap (Diagram 5-5). X4 slides into the vertical passing lane, shading the diagonal. X3 hovers outside the horizontal passing lane, also shading the diagonal. X5 remains at deep safety, preventing the layup, gambling on the "lob" pass to either corner.

A pass over X2's head must be a "lob" if X2 did his job and stayed in the passing lane between 1 and 3. X4 can intercept this pass or at least deflect it. Should X4 get there late and the pass be completed, X4 and X2 trap. X3 drops into the free throw lane, defending the basket, covering the diagonal passing lane. X5 physically plays the basket but mentally shades the vertical passing lane. X1 covers the horizontal passing lane (Diagram 5-5).

Because X5 never leaves the basket area until another teammate can cover for him, the 1-2-1-1 is as safe as a drop-back press can be. X5 must front the low-post strongside attacker when the ball is at the wing or in the corner. If you decide to send X5 out to cover the corner, then X3 or X2 would have to deny the ball into the low post.

The 1-2-2 Drop-Back Press. The 1-2-2 drop-back press allows for both safety and pressure. If you have five medium-sized but quick defenders, this press will make your club championship caliber.

Diagram 5-6 displays the beginning alignment and the initial trap as 1 drives into the perimeter pressure point. X1 stays between 1 and 2, making 1's pass to 2 be lobbed. X2 positions himself between 1 and 3, so that this pass also is lobbed. X3 takes the middle pass away. You want to start X4 and X5 at least as high as the free throw line, higher if they have inordinate quickness and jumping abilities. X4 can easily cover any pass to 3, and X5 covers the "lob" pass to 4 and protects the basket area. Encourage the long "lob" from 1 to the basket area. Either X4 or X5 will snare that pass.

A club that reverses the pass back to 2 can defeat this press, but the pass must be direct, not lobbed. By playing a tall, long-armed bandit at X1, you can prevent this.

Some teams try to pass to 5. When this occurs frequently, you adjust by sinking X1 inside to help. X1 physically plays the diagonal lane to 5, but he remains mentally alert for the direct reverse pass to 2.

If 1 dribbles too far into the perimeter pressure point, near or across the midcourt line, or if 3 breaks there and 1 passes to 3, X1 and X2 trap. X4 does not have to move to cover the vertical passing lane. X5 has the diagonal lane and protects the basket, and X3 does not have to move to deny the horizontal pass (Diagram 5-6).

A pass from 1 to 3 would have X4 and X2 trapping. X5 slides over to cover the low post and the corner pass. X3 races to cover the diagonal and basket area. X1 would shade the horizontal.

You could even rule a third trapping area. A pass from 3 to 6 would mandate X5 and X4 to trap. X3 would have the low post. X1 would slide to weakside rebounding, and X2 would not let a pass go into the high-post region.

If you intend to use four quick defenders and one slow, place the slow defender at either X1 or X5. If you have three exceptionally quick defenders and two ordinary, you have two options available: place the slower defenders at X3 or X5, or place them at X1 and X5. If you have five medium-sized, quick defenders, the 1-2-2 drop-back press was made for you.

Stunts. Your three best stunts for your drop-back press, and they work equally well from either alignment, are laning, hedging, and the run-and-jump exchange. Each will be explained from the 1-2-2 alignment, leaving it to you to adjust the stunts for the other formations.

(A.) Laning. X1 "picks up" 1 as quickly as he receives the ball inbounds (Diagram 5-7). X1 could wait until 1 or 2 has advanced the ball

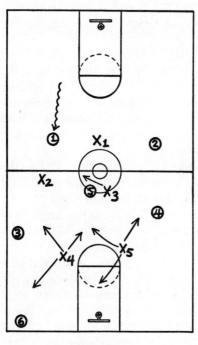

DIAGRAM 5-6

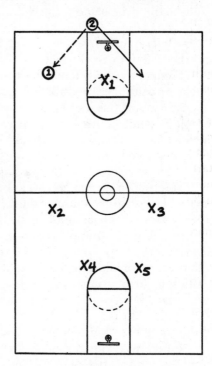

DIAGRAM 5-7

to another predetermined spot. To lane X1 stations himself between 1 and the crosscourt pass receiver. Player 1 must either dribble toward X1, a horizontal move, or pass a high "lob" to 2. If it is far enough upcourt, X3 might steal the "lob." If not, the defense adjusts to the other side of the court.

The main purpose of laning is to keep the ball on one side of the court. This allows X1's teammates to overplay one side of the court earlier and to have a half-step advantage on the next pass.

By alternating where X1 "picks up" 1, you can change the look of your press. You might even have X1 face-guard 1, forcing 2 to pass inbounds to a second best ball handler.

(B.) Hedging. After 1 has been trapped a few times, the art of hedging becomes very real and very usable. Player 1 is being pressured by X1 (Diagram 5-8). X2 drops like he intends to cover 3, but races hard back up to cover 1. Player 1 will usually kill his dribble. X1 must make 1 think he and X2 intend to trap. As soon as 1 stops his dribble, X2 yells "used." X4 covers 3 man-to-man, X5 takes 4, X3 denies 5 the ball, and X1 scampers off to get into the passing lane to 2. If 1 is in frontcourt, the passing lanes need to be covered for five seconds. After five seconds a violation occurs and the defense gets the ball. X2 can help the passing lane defenders by pressuring 1 with his arms swinging, keeping his hands in the same plane as the ball. If 1 picks up his dribble in backcourt, the passing lane defenders need to cover their men for only the amount of time left on the ten-second count. Then a backcourt violation is called, and the defense gets the ball.

Frequently the offense helps out the defense. Player 1 has been taught to pause before dribbling across the time-line and to check the defense. Couple this with 1 having been trapped a few times and it is easy to understand 1's hesitancy. Player 1 will dribble to the perimeter pressure-point area just before midcourt, pick up his dribble, and look for somewhere to throw a pass. At exactly that moment, X2 pressures 1, and X2's teammates close the passing lanes.

You could rule that X1 covers 1 while X2, X3, X4, and X5 cover the passing lanes. Study your personnel, the objectives of your press, and create chaos in 1's ball-handling skills by alternating stunts and presses.

(C.) Run-and-Jump Exchange. Diagram 5-9 shows the simplest of the run-and-jump exchanges, a two-man swap between X1 and X2. Allow a three-man exchange by letting X4 come up to cover 3 with X1 rotating back to assume X4's duties. You should never use more than a three-man rotation and yet stay with your 1-2-2 drop-back zone press. You would confuse your defenders as to their assignments. If you want to use more than a three-man rotation, go man-to-man run-and-jump.

When you run-and-jump exchange, you should have X2 call "jump" or "trap." If 1 picks up his dribble, X2 could even call "used."

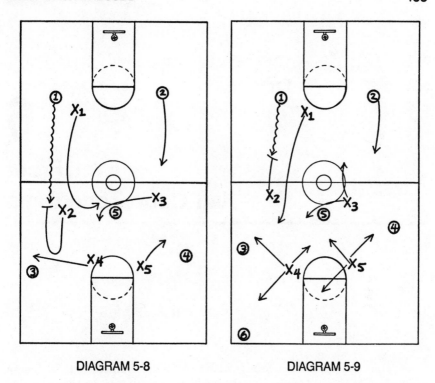

DIAGRAM 5-8   DIAGRAM 5-9

"Jump" and "used" tell X1 to go assume X2's roll and that X2 will become the new X1. "Trap" keeps the same 1-2-2 trapping duties previously explained for every defender.

Because it could confuse the defense as well as the offense, you should have keys that call which maneuver you intend to use. Each defender should know if you intend to "trap," "jump," or "used." In that manner, each can execute his duties quicker and with more confidence. When an exchange of duties is called ("jump" or "used"), the defenders will know ahead of time and be better prepared to anticipate their next assignment.

When you have an experienced ball club that meets the personnel requirements, you might let your players pick and choose as the play develops. This makes for more spontaneity, but it can also confuse X1 and X4.

6

Even Front
Half-Court Zone Traps

Half-court zone traps, regardless of their initial formations, begin with all five defenders in frontcourt. These traps can be extended or contracted at the whim of the coach. They can spread to trap the ball as it crosses the midcourt line; or they can compress to cover only the area from the key to the basket, the area known as the shooting area. Consider your team's quickness and speed against your opponent's ability to move the ball before you decide where to begin your initial trap.

Half-court traps are complete defenses within themselves. They are run continuously, trapping and re-trapping until the offense scores or the defense gets the ball by a turnover or by a defensive rebound. Even when the trap does not steal the ball, it can effectively and perpetually force hurried shots. The fact that half-court traps (called traps instead of presses to distinguish them from their full-court counterparts) are continuous complete defenses separates them from the full-court presses and the drop-back defenses.

Although half-court traps are complete defenses, they can be combined with standard zones or other presses to produce the multiple look. By alternating initial trapping areas, the slides remaining the same, you can confuse offensive attacks, keeping them off-balance. Because the slides are the same regardless of where the trap begins, the defense gains the upper hand in practice preparations. Stunts can even be added to further complicate offensive preparednesss.

THE 2-2-1 HALF-COURT TRAP

Personnel Needed for This Press. Diagram 6-1 illustrates an initial positioning of the 2-2-1 half-court trap, starting at the top of the key. You can extend the trap all the way up to the midcourt line. If you have excellent team quickness or if your opponents do not move the ball well by passing, you would want to make such an extension. Also, if the opponent's top scorer is their best ball handler, extend your press. Now your counterpart must decide whether to keep his best ball handler outside where he cannot score, thus eliminating turnovers but decreasing shooting accuracy; or bring the scorer to the wing or corner positions, admittingly giving more turnovers because of weaker ball-handling.

Whichever you decide, extend or contract, you want the trapping areas and the slides to remain constant. You will want the same personnel to occupy the same spots whether you order spread or congest. For optimum effectiveness, X1 and X2 must be quick, usually guards. If they have size along with quickness, it will make the 2-2-1 trap even more effective. They must possess good judgment. They must realize how the offensive attack is trying to hurt their press: They must know when and where to begin their press, and have patience and know when to wait. Sometimes it is best to be like a cat hiding, waiting for its prey to reach a particular spot before pouncing.

X3 and X4 must be bigger, probably forwards. If they also have quickness and can jump, you will have a championship caliber trap. These two must be aggressive: They must be willing to extend themselves and press with abandonment. Size is the primary characteristic because they provide the trap which closes the passing lane to the basket. This size could prevent a smaller ball handler from finding an open target. They must rebound the weak side, the primary rebounding area.

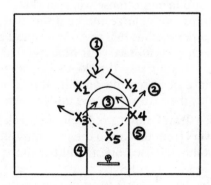

DIAGRAM 6-1

X5 is your smartest player. He must have speed and quickness, yet he needs enough size to be the bottom defender on traps in the corner and to play low-post attackers, usually big men, who receive passes from the wing. Speed is the primary characteristic because X5 must cover from corner to corner.

Duties of Each Position. These will be explained as the ball is moved from one section of the court to another (see section on basic slides of the 2-2-1 half-court trap).

What the 2-2-1 Trap Can Accomplish. Most coaches who teach half-court traps prefer the odd front traps, so offensive teams prepare more for the odd front half-court trap. The even front half-court traps, the 2-2-1 and the 2-1-2, have advantages in preparedness. These advantages cannot be overemphasized. A team that has not drilled and drilled and drilled against a particular trap will lose to that trap. Couple this alignment advantage with the trap's ability to extend and contract, requiring the offense to begin at different points on the court, yet the defense learns only one set of slides and traps; and it becomes easy to see the advantage the defense has over any offensive preparations. An offensive coach must slight or neglect his preparations for the secondary defenses he will face. You know which he will choose, an advantage for your trap.

Beside the obvious team practice accomplishments, there also exist special achievements. An outside shooter can be taken completely out of his range. A team of dribblers or an offense designed to make maximum use of the dribble has no chance of success against a trap. By adjusting your trap, you can also eliminate any advantage a great penetrator has over ordinary zone or man-to-man defenses.

Teams that want a slower tempo should use the spread trap. This usually creates quicker ball movement, and after a few passes, a turnover or a hurried shot. On offense you slow the ball for an excellent shot. Before long your opponent's offense will also slow to your tempo.

Half-court traps can change momentum. After your opponents have scored several possessions in a row, you can call a time-out to try to reverse this trend. Or you can save your time-out and switch to the trap. The wider you spread your trap the slower the offense will attack it. If your opponents have been scoring quickly, spread it; but if they have scored methodically, then trap from the 28-foot marker in.

What the 2-2-1 Trap Cannot Do. It cannot break a stall which places four offensive players from the key to the midcourt line. The attacker on the baseline keeps the defense honest, and the four passers outside can hold the ball the full 32 minutes.

It cannot effectively harm a team of good passers. By proper ball movement, the passers can tire the defense, hurting them both on defense and when they revert to offense. These good passers will also maintain possession until they secure the good high percentage shot without a defender nearby.

The 2-2-1 half-court trap cannot stop a good high-post dribbling penetrator–passer. When this attacker receives the pass from his perimeter teammates, he has virtually free rein inside. Good, solid low-post attackers, who have been schooled in proper posting-up techniques, can hurt the 2-2-1 trap.

Where and When to Use the 2-2-1 Half-Court Trap. Half-court traps as change-up defenses have great merit. Attacking teams must recognize instantly when the change-up begins, otherwise a poor offensive possession will result. When you change-up sporadically, turnovers accumulate, and victory can be traced to violations.

When your opponent decides to hold the ball, the 2-2-1 half-court trap will usually buy you a quick turnover. After gaining the quickie, the offense might be able to hold the ball several seconds on the ensuing possessions. If you have allowed sufficient time, the 2-2-1 trap can gain enough violations and hurried shots to allow you ultimately to win even against a team of good ball handlers. The offensive decision to hold the ball helps the trap. Not only does this offensive decision aid psychologically but the absence of attempts to score allows greater gambling. Half-court traps can work miracles against stalling offensive teams, whether the offense plans to hold the ball from opening tip or to protect a fragile lead late in the game.

Basic Slides of the 2-2-1 Half-Court Trap. Diagram 6-1 illustrates the first trapping area. All the diagrams depicting the 2-2-1 trap will be shown near the scoring area, but the press can be extended to cover the entire frontcourt. Our nomenclature calls the half-court trap the area from the midcourt line to the basket. We further define the 21-foot area from the basket out as trapping the shooting area. You can consult chapter 10 to see different ways of numbering the court so your defenders will know how far downcourt to extend their trap. The 2-2-1 entire half-court trap will be shown by trapping only the shooting areas. X1 and X2, in Diagram 6-1, could just as easily attack the ball as it crosses the midcourt line.

X1 and X2 can drop inside the circle and spring out on a predetermined signal to trap (Diagram 6-1). Their defensive positioning can vary: They can on one possession stay in the passing lanes to the wings, showing the middle passing lane open; and on the next possession, these two defenders can place their bodies to deny any direct pass to the high post, allowing bounce passes around them to the wings.

X3 and X4 must see this trap and read X1 and X2's method of trapping. X3 and X4 can also cover where the attackers are and discount where they are not. For example, in Diagram 6-1, X3 does not have a wing attacker to cover. X3 takes 3 at the high post. X4, if he already knows this will happen, can shade toward 2, a wing attacker. Talking helps, and planning is a must.

X5 must watch 1's eyes. He can determine if 1 intends to throw toward 4 or toward 5.

Diagram 6-2 exhibits the wing trapping responsibilities. X4 stops 2's advance toward the baseline. X2 runs his banana route and helps X4 trap. X5 prevents any pass into the low-post area. X1 defends the high post and X3 has weak side help duties.

Should the ball advance to the corner, X5 prevents the baseline drive, and X4 traps with X5 (Diagram 6-3). X1 covers the high post while X3 still protects the weak side and the basket. X2 drops to cover the low post, the perfect dropping angle for an interception. However, if X2 and/or X1 do not possess physical abilities to prevent passes into the low post, you could alter your lane coverage rules. X3 slides over and covers the low post; X1 drops to the weak side; and X2 remains in the high-post passing lane.

If the ball should go into the low post, you can still trap. If it comes from the wing X5 and X3 trap (Diagram 6-2); X1 drops to protect the basket. If the pass comes from the corner X2 and X3 trap and X1 drops to the basket (Diagram 6-3). This is consistent with all our breakaway coverage rules: Weakside deep defender picks up breakaway dribbler or pass receiver (X3 in both Diagrams 6-2 and 6-3) and the weakside guard defender (X1 in both diagrams) drops to cover the basket area.

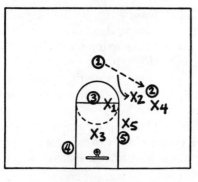

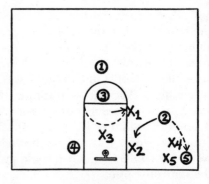

DIAGRAM 6-2   DIAGRAM 6-3

Alternate Slides of the 2-2-1 Half-Court Trap. When you have an exceptional shot blocker at X5, you may want him to stay inside and not go to the corner to trap. You may wish to use these alternate slides. Also, when X1 and X2 do not have the physical characteristics to defend the low post, these alternate slides may be better for your squad.

Diagram 6-4 displays proper coverage with the ball at a wing. X4 and X2 trap the ball. X3 sags to an area just outside the lane but in a straight line between the ball and the basket. X1 covers the horizontal passing lane. X5 defends the basket area. If the ball had advanced to the opposite wing, X1 and X3 would have trapped. X4 would assume X3's duties, and X2 would have done the same slide as X1.

Diagram 6-5 exhibits coverage with the ball in the corner. X3 and X4 trap. X5 denies passes into the low post. X2 places himself between the ball and any high-post attacker. X1 has weakside duties.

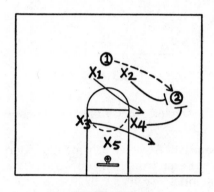

DIAGRAM 6-4

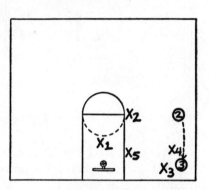

DIAGRAM 6-5

THE 2-1-2 HALF-COURT TRAP

While the 2-2-1 half-court trap's slides are less familiar, the 2-1-2 half-court trap's slides are more commonplace. This fact alone makes the 2-2-1 more attractive to some coaches, and yet to those others who favor the familiar the 2-1-2 remains popular.

Personnel Needed for the 2-1-2. X1 and X2 must be the quick point-guard type (Diagram 6-6). If they happen also to have size, it will make the press that much better.

X3 must possess the best athletic skills. He must have basketball savvy. He needs to have the quickness that X1 and X2 possess. But he must also have size because he will be required to cover inside low-post attackers. X3 must, in essence, be a post defender who has the ability to play point guard.

X4 and X5 can be slow but they must have size. The more quickness they have the further out on the court you can trap. If they have quickness and jumping ability, you have the personnel to develop a championship half-court trap.

Duties of Each Position. Diagram 6-7 depicts the trapping responsibilities of each defender. X1 and X2 trap from the center of court out. X5 and X4 can trap at high wing or help trap in the corner. X3 defends

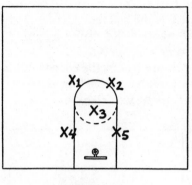

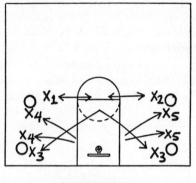

DIAGRAM 6-6   DIAGRAM 6-7

the high post, but he must also trap the corners, preventing any baseline drives.

What the 2-1-2 Trap Can Accomplish. As previously mentioned in the parallel section on the 2-2-1 trap, the even front half-court traps have an advantage in preparedness. Most offensive teams drill in practice against the more popular odd front half-court traps.

An outside shooter can be taken completely out of his range by extending the 2-1-2 trap. A good passing team can be slowed by defending the passing lanes, using loose trapping techniques (see chapter 1). An organized, smooth-working offensive machine can be trapped at different locations on the court: as they cross the midcourt line, at the 28-foot mark, or only inside the shooting areas. This diversity of primary trapping areas can disrupt the timing and the rhythm of the smooth functioning offensive machine. A great penetrator-passer can have his game rendered null and void by the half-court trap.

The 2-1-2 half-court trap can force a quicker tempo. By spreading the trap, methodical teams must be extremely poised or their prepared game tempo will escape them.

All half-court traps can change game momentum. After your opponents have scored several unanswered baskets, a time-out or a change to the 2-1-2 trap will frequently change the momentum (see chapter 10 to find useful signals for calling the traps without using a time-out).

What the 2-1-2 Half-Court Trap Cannot Do. A high post, wing, low post triangular overload gives the 2-1-2 its most trouble. These players, especially when the wing is a good shooter, require X3 to cover too great an area of the court. Easy shots usually result.

A 2-2-1 offensive alignment used as a stall works a hardship on the 2-1-2 trap. When the one in the 2-2-1 runs from the big block to the big block, always appearing on the ballside when a pass goes to a wing, it leaves X3 guarding empty space. A layup could result. If X3 drops too quickly, a flash to the free throw line results in a two-on-one offensive drive situation.

When and Where to Use the 2-1-2 Trap. It is best used as a change-up. When your team employs the 2-1-2 or the 3-2 yo-yo basic zone defenses regularly, the 2-1-2 trap complements well. Sporadic use of the 2-1-2 trap, even when another defense is your basic, pays dividends.

Basic Slides of the 2-1-2 Half-Court Trap. To explain the basic slides of the 2-1-2 trap, we will allow no traps above the free throw line, but trap everything below the free throw line extended (see Diagram 6-8). You can alter this two ways: You could extend the trapping area further out on the court; or you could trap with the two guards in the no trapping area, like in Diagram 6-1 of the 2-2-1 zone trap. The 2-1-2 trap works best when compacted into the area from the baseline to the free throw line.

Diagram 6-9 depicts the trap at a wing. X1 and X4 trap. X3 drops to cover the low post. X5 shades the basket area and is responsible for weakside rebounding. X2 covers the horizontal passing lane. If the ball had been passed down the other sideline, X2 and X5 would have trapped. X3 would still cover low post. X4 would have weakside responsibilities, and X1 would cover the high-post region.

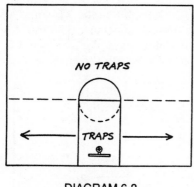

DIAGRAM 6-8

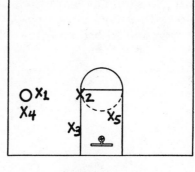

DIAGRAM 6-9

Diagram 6-10 shows the coverage as the pass goes into the corner. X3 stays at low post until he sees the ball fly toward the corner. X3 must arrive as the ball arrives. X4 helps on the trap. X1 drops to high-post coverage, occasionally gambling on an interception on the vertical pass back out. X5 denies a pass to the low post, and X2 has weakside duties. If the ball had been advanced to the other corner, X3 and X5 would have trapped. X4 would have covered the low post. X1 would have weakside duties, and X2 would have denied passes to the high-post area.

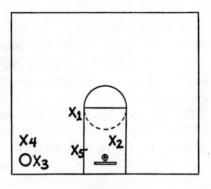

DIAGRAM 6-10

Alternate Slides of the 2-1-2 Half-Court Trap. If X4 and X5 are immobile and X1, X2, and X3 are very quick and aggressive, consider these alternate slides. Diagrams 6-11 and 6-12 display the coverage from the wing and the corner respectively.

Diagram 6-11 illustrates a pass or a dribble to the wing position. X3 prevents further penetration along the vertical. X2 clamps the trap horizontally. X5 denies any pass to the strongside block area, yet he must anticipate any pass going to the corner. X1 hurries to defend the high-post region, and X4 protects the basket while assuming weakside duties.

Diagram 6-12 demonstrates the coverage as the ball advances to the corner. X5 stops any move along the baseline. X3 helps X5 trap. X4 denies any pass into the low post. X2 refuses to allow any pass into the high post, and X1 becomes the weakside defender.

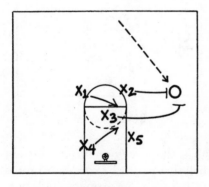

DIAGRAM 6-11

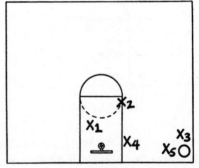

DIAGRAM 6-12

No matter how tough you play your even front half-court trap, whether the 2-2-1 or the 2-1-2, breakdowns will occur, mistakes will be made. When this happens, you must have a pre-drilled plan of presenting the offense another obstacle to scoring. Diagram 6-13 represents the proper recovery coverage regardless of which half-court trap you choose. Letters will be used because the personnel changes depending on whose duties it is to trap and where the breakaway occurred. B, the defender the attacker drove around, follows the dribbler, pressuring him. P, the deepest defender, races to stop the drive. P and B trap. W, the weakside deep defender, comes hard to cover for P, denying any horizontal penetrating pass. H drops to cover the area left by W. T, the original trapper, hustles toward the lane to cover any possible pass.

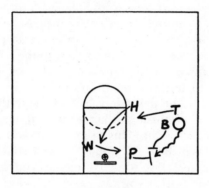

DIAGRAM 6-13

Changing the Pace of the Even-Front Traps. It is easy to change the pace by extending or compressing the initial trap area. You can play it soft out front and trap the ball when it goes to the corner. Or you can trap one side of the court and play regular zone slides on the other.

Any time you trap and put pressure on the passing lanes, action will speed up. It may not result in a turnover or a quick shot but it will force much more ball movement, much greater chance for offensive error. Whether or not the offense puts up a quick shot or passes to get a better one depends more on the offensive objectives than on the defensive pressure.

Stunts can be added to change the tempo. After several trapping possessions, the defense can fake a trap, force the ball handler to pick up his dribble, rotate into the passing lanes, and cover man-to-man. Five seconds of continuous coverage will get a violation. Rotating from the trap into man-to-man can confuse even the best prepared offensive machines.

Combining the half-court with man-to-man and/or regular zone coverage forces opponents to be ever aware. By running zones, for instance, when you score from the field, or the trap when you make or miss a free throw, and man-to-man when you fail to score from the field, you create a multiple defensive look. This multiple look slows down offensive attacks.

Adjustments of the Even-Front Half-Court Traps. Adjustments while trapping can be as simple or as complex as you wish. Instead of trapping the four corners and the wings, you trap only along the baseline, for example. Or you can trap just particular people, such as great shooters only. A nonshooter but a great penetrator can have his game eliminated by judicious use of the trap. Or you can trap one side of the court and play a regular zone on the other.

You can make your game plan much more complicated by combining two different half-court zone traps. The 2-1-2 trap, for example, can be applied only from the free throw line to the baseline. The 1-2-1-1 (see chapter 7) can be used by the same team to create pressure from the midcourt line to the free throw line or even to the baseline. These two presses, acting as one or coupled into a multiple look, create a combination that is difficult to defeat. You must drill your players so the slides will not be as confusing to the defenders as it will be to the attackers.

Stunts add another possible adjustment. Diagram 6-14 shows a run-and-jump into the 2-2-1 trap. This original run-and-jump move could force 1 to pick up his dribble. X2 would take any attacker in the vertical lane. X4 covers the weak side while X5 picks up any player in the post. X3 should pressure 1 with constant arm swinging motions. In five seconds the defense will be awarded the ball. A hurried pass should be stolen and should result in a quick transition basket for the defense. Failing to steal the pass, the defense is still set to begin playing their regular 2-2-1 half-court trap. You have the option of run-and-jump into a man-to-man defense or run-and-jump into the half-court trap on any successful completion of the pass from the dribbling 1.

A gambling attempt at a steal offers another possible adjustment, as shown in Diagram 6-12. With the ball trapped in the corner, X2 could gamble in the vertical reverse passing lane. X1 would then fill the high-post diagonal passing lane. This weakens the weak side so it must be used only in gambling situations or as an occasional change-up.

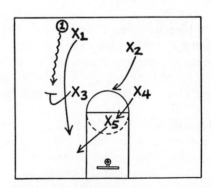

DIAGRAM 6-14

More stunts will be added in the next chapter. With a little imagination you can adjust any stunt to work with any half-court trap's initial alignment.

7

Odd Front
Half-Court Traps

Odd front half-court zone presses are far more popular than their even-front counterparts. The 1-2-1-1, the 1-3-1, and the 1-2-2 have positional advantages that allow the defense to keep more pressure on the ball, to trap more naturally, to keep passes out of the middle, and to prevent dribbling penetration around the perimeter. In each formation, a crosscourt diagonal pass must be covered one-on-one by the opposite wing until trapping help can arrive.

Each press can place their big men up front. By doing this, the big men have less area to run during transition. If you plan to full-court press and you use the big men up front, the half-court trap with big men up front leaves little or nothing new to teach. Short offensive attackers have a difficult time seeing over or around the big defensive men, and it frees the smaller defenders to use their quickness as gap shooters. Your big men, however, must have some quickness or the smaller guard penetrators will drive around the big defenders, putting too much pressure on the basket area.

You can use the bigger players at the deep positions. This makes for better defensive rebounding, and it probably allows for quicker outside pressure. Odd front half-court presses offer greater positional flexibility. In each of the following presses perfect positional personnel will be discussed. They may be altered to coincide with the personnel you have on hand.

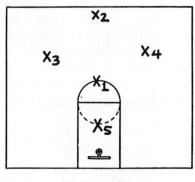

DIAGRAM 7-1

THE 1-2-1-1 HALF-COURT TRAP

Personnel Needed for This Press. Diagram 7-1 displays the alignment. The stronger the player personnel down the middle (X2, X1, and X5), the better the press will be. X2 needs some height, and he needs long arms. He can be the second guard or the small forward. His job requires him to compel lobbed crosscourt passes. X1, the defensive key to the press, must have superior quickness, and he must possess great speed. He has to run from corner to corner yet keep the ball out of the high-post region. X5 should be tall enough to force off-balanced inside shots should the offense successfully get the ball low. Yet X5 must be quick enough to deny passes to either low-post positions. X3 and X4 can have less desirable defensive traits. If both have some size and quickness, the 1-2-1-1 would be almost unbeatable. You could get by with an average X2, but X1 and X5 must be above average.

Duties of Each Position. Only X5 does not trap. He must deny all passes into either low posts; and should a ball get inside, X5 must block the shot attempt or force the shooter to alter his shot. Beside trapping, X1 must keep passes out of the high post yet he must trap the baselines. X2 traps out front and denies passes from the corners to the high-post area. X3 and X4 trap their sides of the court both out front and on the baseline, they rebound when on the weak side, and they shoot the gaps for steals on crosscourt passes.

What This Press Can Accomplish. It can force the opponents into many bad pass situations, compel five-seconds violations, and steal many hurried or poorly thrown passes. It breaks up all stall offenses, including the famous four corners. It ruins patterned, robot-like ball clubs. It tires poorly conditioned teams or teams with few or no reserves. It upsets inexperienced ball clubs. The 1-2-1-1 half-court trap works exceptionally well when you are faced with an overwhelming height disadvantage. It curbs the effectiveness of one or two great players. It slaughters the poor ball handlers. It forces hurried or quick shots, even from the experienced poised players. This trap can even get your offense going.

What This Press Cannot Do. An attacking team that becomes content to hold the ball by placing five players from the free throw line to the midcourt line can hold the ball. But they still must possess adept ball handlers. A team with an excellent high-post penetrator, either by dribble or by pass, can score against the 1-2-1-1. A team that moves the ball around the perimeter quickly can get good corner shots.

Where and When to Use This Trap. The end of any game is a good time to force turnovers or to break a stall. Teams that shoot from certain areas can find those areas closed by the trap. A team with only one good ball handler should be trapped. One good shooter should also be trapped. Teams that pass or dribble poorly must be trapped. Out-of-conditioned teams should face the half-court trap. Set-patterned teams are ineffective against the 1-2-1-1 trap. Inexperienced teams or those who have not drilled against this trap cannot defeat it. On those nights when your offense is sluggish, you should trap to get your offense going.

Basic Slides of the Trap. Diagram 7-2 shows the initial trap as the ball crosses midcourt. X2 and X3 trap while X1 covers the ball side of the high-post attacker. X4 covers the weakside high post. X4, on occasions, can gamble on the crosscourt pass to 2. X5 watches 1 for any indication that he may pass to 5 at the low post.

Diagram 7-3 is an extension of Diagram 7-2. X1 and X3 trap the pass to a cornerman. X5 denies the low post, and X2 denies the high post. X4 has the weakside rebound, or he can gamble on crosscourt diagonal pass from 3 to 2. A completed crosscourt pass requires X4 to

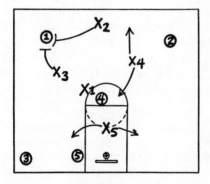

DIAGRAM 7-2

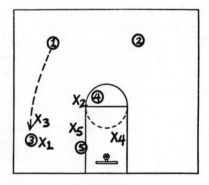

DIAGRAM 7-3

hold the new attacker with the ball until trapping help can arrive. X4 accomplishes this by turning the dribbling attacker outside before he brings the dribbler under control. This delays penetration long enough for X2 or X1 to arrive. If 3 had been stationed at a wing (free throw line extended), there would have been no trap. X3 would have covered 3 while X1 stayed in the passing lane between 3 and the high or low post.

Should 3 drive the baseline into the low post before X1 can get there or should 3 pass to 5 inside, X1 and X5 would trap (Diagram 7-4). X4 denies crosscourt under the basket passes. X2 drops into the middle of the lane, and X3 refuses vertical passes. When the ball is passed back out, the defense recovers and begins again.

Passes down the other side of the floor have the same trapping areas and the same lane coverages. The defensive assignments are merely reversed.

A pass into the high post from out front has X1 playing the attacker one-on-one. X3 and X4 quickly drop to areas about half way down the lane, aiding X5 on coverages into the low-post regions. X2 hustles to help X1 impel the pass back outside from the high post. When the ball is passed back outside, the defense begins again. If the ball is passed from the high post to the baseline corner, X3 or X4 must keep the attacker from shooting or penetrating until X1 can arrive.

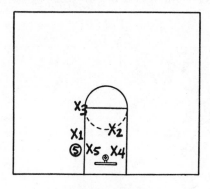

DIAGRAM 7-4

Alternate Slides of the 1-2-1-1 Trap. If you prefer to trap at the wings, you must use an alternate set of slides. To explain these slides, we will go down the opposite side of the court. Diagram 7-5 illustrates the initial trap as the ball crosses midcourt. X2 and X4 trap 2. X1 defends the ball-side high post; and X3 has weakside high-post responsibilities, occasionally gambling for an outside perimeter interception. X5 covers the low-post region, shading the ball side.

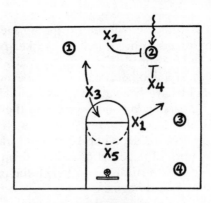

DIAGRAM 7-5

Diagram 7-6 exhibits the wing trapping coverage. X1 and X4 trap 3. X5 denies low post, and X2 defends the high post. X3 stops any crosscourt pass and rebounds the weak side.

Diagram 7-7 continues the coverage into the corner position. X5 and X1 trap. X4 drops into the low-post area. X2 maintains the all-important high-post coverage position, and X3 still has his weakside responsibilities. If X1 were tall enough to defend the low post, you could rule that X4 and X1 exchange duties on passes from the wing into the corner.

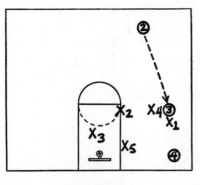

DIAGRAM 7-6

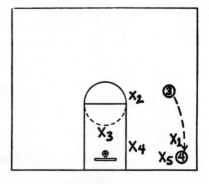

DIAGRAM 7-7

Adjustments of This Trap. Adjustments come in two forms: changing the entire objectives of the press or merely adjusting the press to defense particular offensive goals. The former is achieved by changing presses or entering into a stunt or changing the game's defensive tempo. The latter merely requires you to change your press minutely.

To change a press minutely you can pick out only certain attackers to trap. Trapping a good shooter or an excellent dribbling penetrator while letting the others face only a zone is an illustration. It is best for the opponent's stronger guard to have possession of the ball because he will feel he can dribble through your double-team. It also places weaker attackers trying to move without the basketball. Also, it frequently takes the strongest player, the penetrating guard, out of the offense with the first trap.

You may want to change the look of your press by trapping the right side and playing zone on the left or vice versa. You may decide to trap the baseline corners but nowhere else. There are many ways you can adjust your press without changing its purposes.

You can also change the objectives of your press; Diagram 7-8 offers one way. You begin by laning the ball, appearing to set your trap. Then X3 races at 1 as he dribbles across the time line. X2 also hedges toward 1 before retreating, appearing to help X3 trap. Player 1 has been trapped several times already. He also has received offensive instructions to get rid of the ball before the trap clamps. Player 1 picks up his dribble. X2 guards the first attacker around the perimeter right of X3. X4 picks up the second attacker around the perimeter right of X3. X5 defends the first attacker around the perimeter left of X3. X1 covers the remaining attacker. These match-up rules give each defender an assigned offensive player. Any completed pass from 1 puts the defenders into a man-to-man defense. If the defenders can prevent a completed pass for five seconds, a violation occurs and the defense regains possession of the ball. This stunt also works with the other traps of this chapter. The stunts described in the parallel sections in this chapter will work with the 1-2-1-1 trap, giving the coach many ways to change the aims of his press.

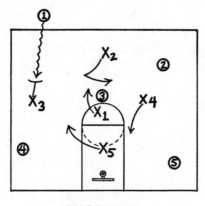

DIAGRAM 7-8

Instead of rotating into man-to-man defense on completion of the above pass, you can stay in your 1-2-1-1 trap. The half-court trap can be as simple or as complex as you wish.

THE 1-3-1 HALF-COURT TRAP

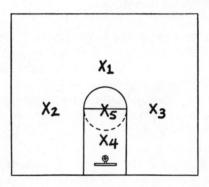

DIAGRAM 7-9

Personnel Needed for This Trap. X1 must be quick and possess good anticipation (Diagram 7-9). He must have the courage to cover the high-post area. He should have quick hands. X2 and X3 have the same duties, but X2 should be slightly quicker while X3 should be a better rebounder. Size helps at both of these positions. Quickness and speed are secondary requirements. X5 must be very quick and very active. He alone keeps the ball out of the middle. If he cannot do this, the 1-3-1 trap cannot be effective. X5 must possess size and strength. His duties require inside defense and rebounding. He must be adept at denying low-post passes. Although you could get away with a big slow rebounder at X5, the quicker and more agile he is the better your trap will be. X4 must have size and speed: size because he covers inside and rebounds the strong-side when a shot is taken from a guard position, and speed because he must cover from corner to corner. Quickness is a secondary requirement for X4.

Duties of Each Position. X1's first job is to direct the ball toward one of the wings, away from the center of the court. He traps with the ballside wing. When a pass goes to the corner, X1 covers the passing lane into the high post. X2 and X3 have the same duties, just on opposite sides of the court. They play between the ball and the attacker behind them, laning it, as the ball comes up the court. The opposite wing, the weak side, drops toward the basket to secure rebound position. X2 and X3, when on the ball side, also trap in the corners. X5 alone keeps the ball out of the middle. He will get help from X1 at the high post and from X4 at the low post. X5 must always stay between the ball and the basket at all times. When the ball is in the corner, X5 must deny all passes into the low-post area. X4 begins at the low post on the ball side. On passes to the corner, X4 traps with a wing. He must always prevent the baseline drive.

What This Press Can Accomplish. It will take patterned ball clubs out of their practiced game plans. It causes offensive teams to rush their perimeter jump shots. Poor passing or poor penetrating ball teams will have little success against the 1-3-1 half-court trap. This trap, expecially when played in the shooting area, can become a ball-hawking, pass-intercepting aggressive defense.

What This Press Cannot Do. It cannot break stalls, nor will it disrupt slow-down tactics. In fact, the further this press moves from the basket area, the less effective it becomes. A well-designed attack, using expert ball handling and passing, can easily get the good jump shot. However, patience and poise must still be an offensive trademark. The 1-3-1 trap tries to panic the offense into a hurried shot. Offenses that will not rush themselves will defeat the 1-3-1 trap. Teams with a good, big, quick inside penetrator-passer will hurt the 1-3-1 trap.

Where and When to Use This Trap. The 1-3-1 trap should be used near the basket. Occasionally, as a change of pace, it might be extended outward near midcourt. The 1-3-1 trap should never be used possession after possession after possession. It is all right to use it several possessions in a row then discard it for the remainder of the quarter, then reactivate it for several possessions before discarding it again. Unlike the 1-2-1-1 or the 1-2-2, the 1-3-1 trap is not a full-game defense, but it works extremely well as a change-up defense. When behind late in a game, the 1-3-1 trap is almost useless. It cannot break the opponent's stall; and by spreading your 1-3-1 trap, you open penetrating passing lanes for easy baskets. Early game use of the 1-3-1 trap is highly recommended; it usually results in a few quick steals. When your opponents are driving well against your team defense, switch to the 1-3-1 trap for a few possessions. It will stop the opponent's driving game.

Basic Slides of the 1-3-1 Trap. Diagrams 7-10 and 7-11 display the coverages as the ball moves down the left defensive side of the court. Symmetrical traps and lane coverages occur as the ball moves down the right defensive side.

X1 and X2 trap 1 (Diagram 7-10). X5 covers the high post, keeping the ball away from 5 yet staying between the ball and the basket. X3 drops to prevent the lob pass to 4 and to secure weakside rebounding position. X3 can occasionally gamble for an interception of the pass from 1 to 2. X4 covers the low-post strong side. He would be above the low-post attacker. He never goes to the corner until the pass is directed there.

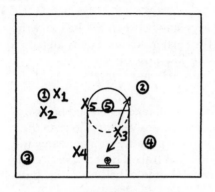

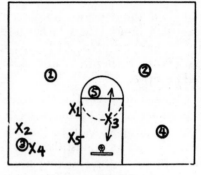

DIAGRAM 7-10   DIAGRAM 7-11

When the ball is passed to the corner, X4 and X2 trap it (Diagram 7-11). X5, keeping between the ball and the basket, slides to cover the low post. X1 prevents a pass from 3 to the high-post region. X3 slides up a step or so when he sees an effective trap by X4 and X2. This allows X3 to intercept the skip pass from 3 to 2. X3 need not worry about the weakside rebound after the trap is set.

If 3 drives by X4, X4 and X5 would trap. X1 drops to the middle of the lane for the diagonal pass. X2 sags to cover the vertical pass, and X3 denies the horizontal pass underneath the basket.

The gambling option is also available. Using Diagram 7-11, X1 slides out into the passing lane from 3 to 1. X3 covers the high-post lane. This coverage, however, is very dangerous and should be used sparingly.

Alternate Slides of the 1-3-1 Trap. Diagrams 7-9, 7-10, and 7-12 show alternate sets of slides. Diagram 7-9 depicts the original 1-3-1 alignment. Diagram 7-10 shows the coverage from out front. Diagram 7-12 exhibits the alternate slide as the ball is passed from out front to the corner. These slides require more gambling, leaving the middle area unprotected for a longer time.

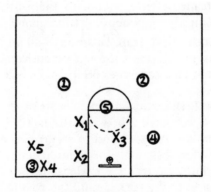

DIAGRAM 7-12

X4 and X5 trap 3 on the pass to the corner (Diagram 7-12). X2 slides into the low-post passing lane, and X1 hustles into the high-post passing lane. Because of the direction of these slides, both X2 and X1 are rotating into the perfect interception angles. They certainly should deflect any pass they cannot intercept. X4 and X5 can help by racing to their trap with their hands high, forcing the slower lob or bounce pass.

You need a recovery for the low-post area should X2 get there late. X3 comes hard to stop 5 (Diagram 7-13). X2 helps trap with X3. X1 has the perfect rotation angle to intercept a pass from 5 to 4. X5 hurries into the middle of the lane, and X4 takes away the vertical passing lane back out to 1. On passes back outside X4 assumes the duties originally belonging to X1. X1 now has X3's original responsibilities, and X3 is now the new X4. X2 and X5 still have their initial assignments.

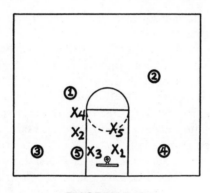

DIAGRAM 7-13

These alternate slides are more dangerous, but they will also produce more steals. Because they are slightly different from the ordinary, offensive teams must prepare specially for them. When all the defenders learn the proper rotations, this alternate 1-3-1 is a very tough, aggressive, hustling defense of its own. Of course it can be taught as a stunt from the more sound basic slides.

Adjustments from the 1-3-1 Trap. Adjustments require the mental flexibility of the coach. Frequently you must adjust your trap to take advantage of the style of offense of your next opponent. This requires stunts created by you, drills provided by you, and drilling your players until they can perform the defense automatically. Such adjustments, however, are never as good as the ones taught for the full year (like the parallel sections of this chapter dealing with the 1-2-1-1 and the 1-2-2). For the sake of completeness let's create some defensive stunts for our next opponent's offense.

Diagram 7-14 illustrates an offense with no high post. It is designed to leave X5 guarding space, giving the offense a 5 on 4 advantage elsewhere. The offense has their best shooter, 3, stationed in one of the

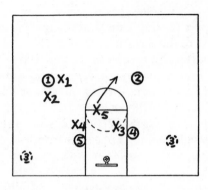

DIAGRAM 7-14

corners. They also have their two best rebounders, 4 and 5, in the primary rebound areas.

To plan an adjustment, you eliminate X5 guarding space. X4 and X3 let X5 know where 3 is. If 3 is opposite the ball, X5 gets in the passing lane between 1 and 2. X4 has 5 at the low post, and X3 defends 4 at the weakside low post (Diagram 7-14). If 1 successfully passes to 2 or if he finds 3, you run your basic slides. Most likely, the offense must adjust so 1 can have a passing lane available. You have adjusted, taking the offense out of their intended game plan.

If 3 is on the ball side, same side as 1, X4 slides out to intercept passes from 1 to 3, X5 has 5 at strongside low post, and X3 has 4 at weakside low post. This impels the pass from 1 to 2, the line of least resistance. X3 and X1 now trap 2. X5 stops the quick pass to 4 before sliding out to cover the passing lane from 2 to 1. X2 covers 5, and X4 has 4 (Diagram 7-14). Now you have the same coverage as before, only on the opposite side of the court. The offense must move to create a passing lane for 2. Your adjustment is very minor because you still have your basic slides, but it has forced the offense out of their practiced plans. You can create these types of adjustments from any basic alignment.

THE 1-2-2 HALF-COURT TRAP

Personnel Needed for This Press. X1 must have quickness. If he also has size, it will make the press that much better (Diagram 7-15). He will probably be your offensive point guard. X2 should be your next best defender. He should also have quickness and some size. Quickness is more important than size, but X2 must have some toughness because he will have to rebound on the weak side. X2 is an ideal spot for your number two offensive guard. X3, probably your small forward, should have the same characteristics as X2. Size is more important than

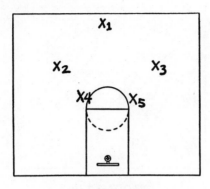

DIAGRAM 7-15

quickness for X3. X4 must have size, and he must possess above-average speed and quickness. He must also be rugged enough to defense the low post and to rebound inside. This is the spot for your offensive power forward. X5 can be your slowest and biggest defender, probably a center type. But the quicker X5 is the better your press will become. He, too, must be strong enough to defense the low post and to rebound inside. You could invert the personnel, letting X1 be the center, X2 and X3 be the forwards, and X4 and X5 be the guards. But in this case you would need five quick defenders. You would also want to use the alternate slide (Diagram 7-19) instead of the basic slides (Diagrams 7-16, 7-17, and 7-18).

Duties of Each Position. X1 begins the press by forcing the ball from the center of the court to one side. Once there, X1 and the ballside wing would trap. If the ball gets to the free throw line extended or below, X1 must have the ability to defend the high-post region. X2 and X3 have the same duties, just on opposite sides of the court. The strongside wing,

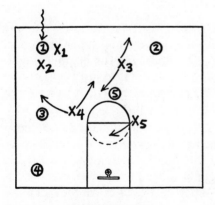

DIAGRAM 7-16

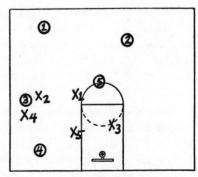

DIAGRAM 7-17

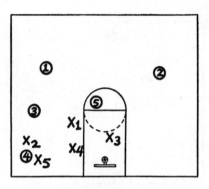

DIAGRAM 7-18

X2 or X3, traps the ball at the guard and the wing positions. When the ball is trapped in the corner, the ballside wing traps while the ballside deep defender defends the low-post region. The weakside wing, X2 or X3, acts as a gap shooter while the ball is trapped out front, and he performs as a weakside rebounder on traps from the free throw line extended to the baseline. The deep defenders, X4 and X5, must act as interceptors on traps set out front. One traps at the free throw line extended while the other defends the low post. One traps when the ball goes into the corner, and the other defends the low post.

What This Press Can Accomplish. This trap runs the full course of defensive accomplishments. It can break a stall, serve as your basic defense, or be used in a multiple defensive plan. This defense is solid enough to be used the entire game, varying the points of pressure and the gambling tactics. There is not anything that the 1-2-2 trap cannot accomplish.

What This Press Cannot Do. The 1-2-2 half-court trap is versatile. This versatility allows the 1-2-2 trap to accomplish whatever you set as your objectives.

Where and When to Use This Trap. This trap may be used at any time during the game. In fact, it may be used during the entire game. The press can expand or contract at your whim. You can begin it at half-court for a few possessions. Then you could limit it to just the shooting area, from the baseline to the free throw line extended. It is, however, more effective when used farther out on the court.

Basic Slides of the 1-2-2 Trap. Diagrams 7-16, 7-17, and 7-18 depict the basic slides of the 1-2-2 trap as the ball moves down the left defensive side of the court. X1 and X2 trap at the guard position (Diagram 7-16). X3 defends the pass into the diagonal lane, but he can gamble for interceptions in the horizontal lane. When X4 sees X1 turn the ball to his side of the court, X4 moves up the lane to cover the vertical passing lane. X4 hopes to encourage 1 to throw a long lob pass. You must decide who is to cover this long lob pass, X4 or X5. If X4 drops, X5 guards the basket. If X5 is to gamble for the interception on the pass from 1 to 4, X4 switches positions with X5 and X4 now is responsible for the basket area. This latter coverage corresponds to the rules of the basic slide.

X3, X4, and X5, the interceptors, and the gap shooters, key the eyes of the attacker with the ball. They jab step toward the next area the ball handler looks at. All three move positively. They don't hesitate. The trappers, X1 and X2 in Diagram 7-16, must move toward their new assignments as 1 releases the pass. This type of movement keeps the offense from gaining a numerical advantage.

Diagram 7-17 continues the movement from Diagram 7-16. As the ball is passed from 1 to 3, X4 holds 3 until X2 arrives to double-team. X1 plays the horizontal passing lane; X3 drops to weakside defense; X4 covers the low post, shading the vertical passing lane.

Diagram 7-18 completes the rotation. X5 and X2 trap the corner. X4 drops to low post while X1 and X3 continue their previous coverage. Of course, if the ball gets to the low post before X4 arrives, X3 and X4 would trap. X1 would drop to the basket area. X5 would take the high-post area and X2 would hustle into the lane. Also, the gambling stunt is available in Diagram 7-18. X1 would cover the pass back out to 3, and X3 would deny the pass to 5. The weak side is left completely open. This stunt is dangerous defensively and should not be used often.

Alternate Slides of the 1-2-2 Trap. You would not want to change the slides in Diagrams 7-16 and 7-17. Your alternate slide is available in Diagram 7-18.

If X2 and X3 were big and strong enough to deny low-post passes, you could change the coverage of Diagram 7-18 to the coverage shown in Diagram 7-19. X5 and X4 would trap. This would be especially appealing if X5 and X4 were your guards, if you were using the inverted coverage discussed earlier. X2 covers the low post, and X1 denies the high post. X3 has weakside defensive and rebounding responsibilities.

Adjustments from the 1-2-2 Trap. The parallel sections of this chapter (1-2-1-1 and 1-3-1) also work with the 1-2-2. This section explains a run-and-jump stunt, which will also work for the 1-2-1-1 and the 1-3-1 traps. By no means are these the only three workable stunts for the odd front half-court traps. The adjustments are limited only by your imagination.

Diagram 7-20 shows the run-and-jump from the 1-2-2 half-court trap. X1 pressures 1 into dribbling hard into the frontcourt. X2 runs directly at 1's dribbling shoulder, yelling "trap," "jump," or "used." If "trap," you have the slides and the coverages of Diagram 7-16. If "jump,"

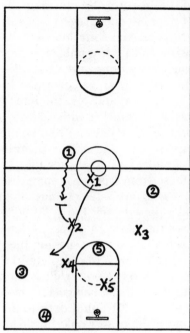

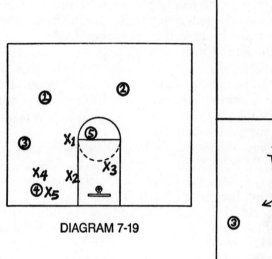

DIAGRAM 7-19

DIAGRAM 7-20

X2 and X1 trade duties and responsibilities unless X4 also enters the rotation. When X4 enters the run-and-jump, X1 assumes X4's duties. X2 becomes the new X1, X4 the new X2, and X1 the new X4. If 1 picks up his dribble and X2 yells "used," you would need a match-up coverage rule: X1 would take the first attacker around the perimeter left of X2; X4 would take the second attacker around the perimeter left of X2; X3 would cover the first attacker around the perimeter right of X2; and X5 would defend the remaining attacker. This means X2 blankets 1, trying to force a bad pass, keeping his hands in the plane of the ball. In Diagram 7-20, X1 would cover 3, X4 would defend 4, X3 would deny 2 the ball, and X5 would guard 5. If 1 cannot successfully pass within five seconds, a violation occurs and the defense gets the ball. If a pass is successful, you have two options available: You could continue your 1-2-2 half-court trap; or you could switch to a man-to-man defense for that possession.

8
Hybrid Half-Court Zone Traps

Almost every year a unique but successful half-court zone trap emerges from the fertile mind of a basketball coach. Frequently it is conceived in desperation but ultimately proves itself beyond expectations. Other coaches in future seasons will attempt to copy the creative trap, but it will never work as well. Why? They do not have the personnel to make the hybrid zone trap successful. Even the originator of the creative trap will see it fail when his material changes. Easily the most important ingredient in a hybrid trap is the personnel.

Is it worth the mental effort to find the perfect trap for your special blend of personnel? The answer is an emphatic *yes*. If you find the exact combination, your trap will have an overwhelming advantage—especially down the tournament trail. Practice your trap daily all season long. Your ideal mixture will make your trap as solid as any defense you could use. Your seasonal opponents will get only a few hours to prepare for your trap; if it is tournament time, they might have only minutes in preparation. Your trap will win.

Be careful! Be wise enough to recognize that your trap may be only a one-season defense instead of a career one. Hybrid traps are presented not only for completeness but also in the hope they will help you see how you can create traps to match your unique material.

THE 1-1-2-1 HALF-COURT TRAP

The 1-1-2-1 trap borders on being a staple instead of a hybrid. When Fran Webster was the defensive master, the University of Pittsburgh used a 1-1-2-1 trap successfully for many years. Of course, they could recruit to fill their needs. It was the zone trap part of their now famous Amoeba System.

Diagram 8-1 depicts the original alignment of the 1-1-2-1. The shaded areas mark the ideal trapping spots. You could drop your trap back to the 28-foot marker or even the scoring area. The ellipses around X2 shows the area he is responsible for should X1 trap with X5 or X4 out front.

Guard X1 serves as the chaser. He is the smaller and quicker of your two guards. He is ideally your point guard on offense. He must have good lateral movement and possess lots of stamina. His job is to force the offensive ball handler into the trap areas (the shaded areas in Diagram 8-1). He wants to force the ball to the sidelines, making the dribbler handle the ball with his off-hand. X1 then teams with X5 or X4 to set the trap, depending on the side of the court the ball is on. Should the ball handler pass the ball to a player in front of X4 or X5 instead of dribbling it there, X2 would trap with X5 or X4 and X1 would assume the duties of X2. In other words, X1 and X2 must be interchangeable. They must possess virtually the same characteristics.

Guard X2, however, needs to be a little taller or at least a good jumper. He must stay in front of any high-post attacker as the dribbler approaches frontcourt. Otherwise he is a carbon copy of X1.

Wings X4 and X5 must be excellent trappers. They must have size so they can prevent a ball handler from seeing an opening underneath the basket. They double-team with X1 and X2 out front and X3 along the baseline. They must be tall so they can discourage passes into the low-

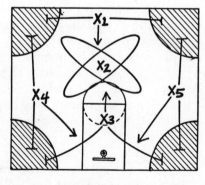

DIAGRAM 8-1

post area and so they can rebound the weak side. X4 should be quicker than X5, but X5 should be the better rebounder.

X3 must be the quickest of your big men. He must possess excellent anticipation. He needs speed because he will cover from sideline to sideline. He must have strength because he frequently has inside defensive responsibilities.

The arrows in Diagram 8-1 disclose each defender's trapping responsibilities. X1 traps outside or takes over X2's duties. The ellipses show X2's movements. But X2 might become X1, so X1 and X2 must know both duties. X5 and X4 trap outside and in the corners. X4 and X5 also rebound the weak side. X3 has inside duties as well as trapping both corners.

Diagram 8-2 displays a trap at the high guard corner. X1 and X5 trap. If 1 had passed to a teammate instead of dribbling into frontcourt, X2 and X5 would have trapped. X1 and X2 would have exchanged duties. X1 stays with the ball on dribbles; on passes X2 takes the pass receiver and X1 drops into the high post.

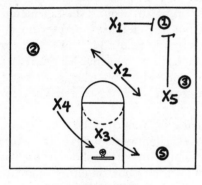

DIAGRAM 8-2

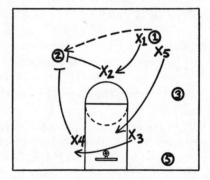

DIAGRAM 8-3

X2, in Diagram 8-2, defends the high-post area while X3 takes the strongside vertical lane. The farther the trap out front the more X3 can gamble. A trap in the shooting area would force X3 to cover the low-post area and gamble less. X4 has weakside responsibilities.

Diagram 8-3 shows the crosscourt pass from 1 to 2. X2 and X4 set the trap. X3 rotates across the lane into the strongside low post and the new vertical passing lane. X5 sinks into the weakside rebound area, and X1 defends the high post but shades the horizontal passing lane.

Diagram 8-4 continues Diagram 8-3. The pass goes from guard to wing position. X5 and X3 trap. X4 covers the low post but shades the vertical passing lane. X2 drops to the weak side while X1 refuses passes into the high post.

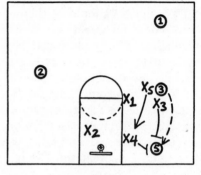

DIAGRAM 8-4   DIAGRAM 8-5

Diagram 8-5 finishes the complete sequence. As 3 passes to 5, X3 and X4 trap. X5 drops to defend the low post. X1 and X2 can help cover the low post until X5 can arrive. Once X5 is in place and the trap has been set by X3 and X4, X1 can gamble on passes around the perimeter.

When the ball reaches the baseline, the defense operates on all ensuing passes with the same rotations that were used in the 1-3-1 trap (see chapter 7). X4 is the baseline runner. X3 is the wing. X2 or X1 is a wing and the other one is the point, depending on who is weakside rebounder when the pass goes into the corner. X5 is the center. The trap is continuous.

These are by no means the only basic slides of the 1-1-2-1 half-court zone trap. There are probably as many excellent basic slides as there are coaches who teach the 1-1-2-1. When teaching any of the slides, you must demand that the defense hustle back down the floor, on either made or missed shots, to set up and prevent the fast break. They force the ball to the perimeter and out of the key area. X1 and X2 must use good coordinated movement. Pressure must always be placed on the ball handler, usually double-teaming pressure. You never want these trappers to reach and grab. This results in a foul. The steals will come off the intercepted passes. These traps will virtually eliminate the attackers from running their usual or most practiced offense. Defenders away from the trap must stay alert and protect all passing lanes. Alertness and aggressiveness are the two most basic elements observed in all championship teams.

Like all traps, the 1-1-2-1 works after field goals, after foul shots, made or missed, for short intervals of time alternating with another defense, or for the entire game. It is a complete defense within itself.

The 1-1-2-1 half-court trap works against poor ball-handling teams, against a tall or a slow team, against the deliberate ball-control team, and against the stall. It works best when not overextended. A small floor is a perfect spot for it. Also, if it is late in a game and you need possession of the ball, the 1-1-2-1 will usually get it for you.

THE 1-1-3 HALF-COURT TRAP

The 1-1-3 half-court trap is kin to the 1-1-2-1 in part but very different in many areas. To run this trap effectively, you must have two extremely quick and fast guards, X1 and X2 in Diagram 8-6. If you have quickness inside, you would probably be better off with a regular trap. X3, X4, and X5 do not have to be quick or fast. In fact, they can be slow.

Because of the nature of this defense, you will want to teach it in two stages. Stage I involves the guard play, and Stage II revolves around the big men.

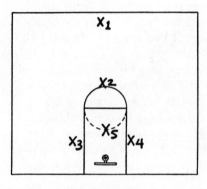

DIAGRAM 8-6

Stage I

Guard X1 must be your quickest defender. He covers the dribbler who crosses midcourt with the ball. He goes with the dribbler until the ball is passed. X2 moves out to guard the pass receiver, and X1 slides inside the key, becoming the new X2. As long as the dribbler dribbles, X1 maneuvers to force the reverse dribble. X2 anticipates the reverse dribble. When X2 sees the reverse dribble begin, he hustles to the ball and helps X1 trap the dribbler.

X2 begins in the middle of the floor, just inside the top of the key. While there, X2 fronts the high post. On a pass to a perimeter player, X2 goes to cover the pass and X1 races inside to front the high post.

Stage II

X3 and X4 play as if they were forwards in a regular 2-3 or 2-1-2 zone, but they can stunt by using man-to-man principles. For example, the strongside forward can deny the ball to a wing. This requires the weakside forward to help on all backdoor cuts on the strong side. This adheres closely to basic man-to-man defensive principles. If the strongside forward has two men in his area, a low-post attacker and a wing for example, the strongside forward plays between them but shades the inside attacker. When the ball comes into the forward area, the strongside forward races out to the ball and the center drops to the low-post coverage strong side. Also, the guards are involved in this maneuver. The guard who had been covering high post races out to help the strongside forward trap the ball. The guard covering the passer breaks inside to front the high post. The center fronts the low post, and the weakside forward has weakside responsibilities.

X5 covers the lane area from the foul line to the baseline, denying the ball to any cutter in the lane. When the ball is out front, X5 has help in defending the high post (the other guard). When the ball is picked up by a forward, X5 must sink quickly to front the low post.

Let's use Diagram 8-7 to talk about the above rules. X1 forces 1 to pass or reverse dribble. If 1 reverses his dribble, X2 would help X1 trap. If 1 passes to 2, X1 would go pick up (same as in the run-and-jump). But if 1 passes to 2 before reversing his dribble, X2 would go cover 2, trying to force 2 to reverse dribble, while X1 helps on high-post coverage. In other words, there would be no trapping above the free throw line extended except in cases of the reverse dribble.

If 1 passed to 3, X3 would slide out to cover 3 (Diagram 8-7). X2 would also hurry to help X3 trap. X5 would drop to low post and front 5. X1 hustles to the high-post area and keeps 4 from receiving a pass. The press continues.

Should 3 drive by X3 or get a pass into 5, X3 and X5 trap. X4 denies any horizontal under the basket pass, and X1 drops into the

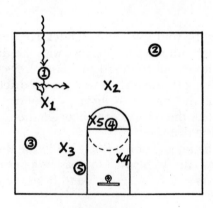

DIAGRAM 8-7

middle of the lane. X2 covers the vertical passing lane, placing himself at least even with the ball, preferably inside of the ball. This is the same consistent coverage of penetration in all the other half-court traps (see chapters 6 and 7).

The 1-1-3 is a little different from the other traps. Although it traps the ball and zones the passing lanes, it is more spontaneous than structured. Defenders must read and react, calling for a little more savvy from your defenders.

Like all traps, it can be run an entire game—even an entire season—without fear of failure. However, it will never reach the popularity enjoyed by the more staple traps.

THE STROTUM TRAP

The Strotum Trap also consists of two parts: the inside two and the outside three. It can begin from a 1-2-2, a 2-1-2, or a 1-1-1-2 alignment. It can also allow the outside three to play man-to-man and the inside two to play zone.

Phase I

Phase I explains the inside two's duties. This is best done using the Strotum Drill. As you (the coach) pass to 3 in Diagram 8-8, X5 goes out to cover the corner. He will receive double-team help from an outside defender (explained later). As X5 goes out to cover 3, he pulls X4 over with him. X5 prevents the baseline drive by 3; X4 prevents any pass into the low-post 5. Should 3 reverse the pass to you, X4 would slide over to cover 4 and X5 would come back inside to cover 5. As long as the ball remains outside the dotted line (Diagram 8-8), X4 and X5 are responsible for the two low-post positions. As coach, you must determine where

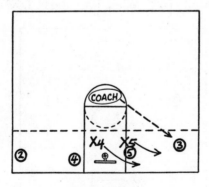

DIAGRAM 8-8

you will place this imaginary dotted line: The quicker X4 and X5 are the farther you can extend it outward from the basket. X4 and X5 stay on the high side of 4 and 5. When you reverse the pass to 2, X4 races out to cover the corner and X5 fronts 4 at the low post. X4 will receive double-team help from a perimeter defender.

Phase II

Phase II deals with perimeter rules. The three outside defenders can start man-to-man, 1-1-1, 2-1, or 1-2. Outside the dotted line (Diagram 8-8), two of these perimeter defenders will trap the ball; the other defends the high post. In this manner the ball is trapped, the high post defended, the strongside low post defended (see Phase I), and the weakside low-post area protected. When the pass goes from a strongside position to the strongside corner, the closest outside defender traps with the Strotum Drill defender. The next closest perimeter defender races to high post to prevent a pass from the corner to the high post. The farthest outside defender from the ball drops to play the weakside low post.

When a pass goes from strongside to the weakside corner, the high-post defender goes to trap with the Strotum Drill defender, X4 in Diagram 8-9, if the pass went from 1 to 4. The inside trapper, X1 in Diagram 8-9, races to high-post defense, and the outside trapper, X3, races to weakside duties. In Diagram 8-9, a pass from 1 to 4 would have X4 and X2 trapping, X5 denying the ball to the low-post strong side, X1 denying the ball to the high-post strong side, and X3 dealing with weakside responsibilities.

Coupling Phase I with Phase II you will always have the ball trapped, the high post and the low post fronted, and the weakside duties covered. Diagram 8-9 offers an example of traps outside and inside the dotted line. X1, X2, and X3 represent perimeter defenders and X4 and X5 perform the Strotum Drill. While 1 has the ball, X1 and X3 trap. X2,

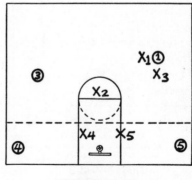

DIAGRAM 8-9

the other outside defender, covers the high-post region. X4 has the weakside low post and X5 the strongside low post. X5 could gamble on an errant pass to 5, and X2 could overplay horizontal passes from 1 to 3.

If 1 passed to 3 (Diagram 8-9), X2 would hurry out to trap with X1. X3 would drop quickly to defend the high-post region. X4 and X5 still play the inside two low-post block positions.

A pass from 1 to 5 puts the ball below the dotted line (Diagram 8-9). X5 would race out to cover 5, preventing the baseline drive. X3 would help X5 trap 5. X4 runs the Strotum Drill, coming over to cover the strongside low post. X2 drops to weakside low post, and X1 would cover the high-post region. Coverage continues until the defense recovers the ball or the offense scores.

Obviously X4 and X5 are too slow to play man-to-man or an ordinary half-court trap. Their lack of individual skills is the reason you considered this press. The better they are the farther out on the court you can draw your imaginary line. Should X4 and X5 improve individually down the year's practice sessions, you could extend your press by placing the dotted line farther downcourt.

X1, X2, and X3 must be quick and fast. They must understand good basketball strategy or be capable of learning it quickly. They must learn which are responsible for trapping and which will have passing lane coverages.

The Strotum Press allows great diversitivity. You can run the regular Strotum Press, or you can have three players play man-to-man and two men zone, or you can defend with a match-up zone. You can also stunt in an unlimited number of ways—a simple man-to-man run-and-jump stunt, for example.

THE MATCH-UP HALF-COURT TRAP

Why teach a match-up zone trap instead of a basic zone trap? Because you can pick up your opponents with a one-on-one coverage in a match-up, your opponents will probably figure you are in a man-to-man defense and they will run their man-to-man attack, especially if you continually change from a man-to-man to a zone or from a zone to a man. Also, if you are known for a half-court zone trap, offensive teams frequently back off just before crossing the time line to set up their offensive attack formation. The match-up zone trap will not allow the offensive team to hesitate to get organized before crossing the time line.

It does not matter what you choose as your initial alignment. All match-ups begin with one-on-one coverage. Your alignment begins in the same form as the offensive formation. This is the purpose of the match-up. We will discuss the match-up half-court trap from a 1-3-1

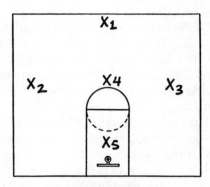

DIAGRAM 8-10

formation (Diagram 8-10). Your rules may differ slightly from these but your rules must be complete and cover two important points: who do your defenders match initially; and who is responsible for the traps, the passing lanes, and safety.

Rules for X1

1. X1 should be your point guard, your quickest and best defender.
2. X1 picks up the ball handler well before he reaches half-court and plays him man-to-man, pushing the dribbler to the outside.
3. X1 traps when the ball is located in Sections A or D (Diagram 8-11). He traps from the inside of the court.
4. X1 defends the high-post area when the ball is in Sections B, C, E, or F (Diagram 8-11).

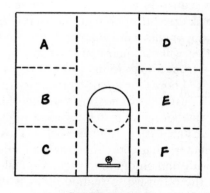

DIAGRAM 8-11

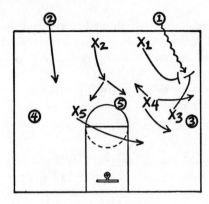

DIAGRAM 8-12

Rules for X2

1. X2 is your second smallest and quickest defender. He is probably your second guard.
2. X2 picks up the first attacker around the perimeter left of X1. X2 guards this attacker even when he is still in backcourt. When this happens the zone is in a 2-1-2 alignment (see Diagram 8-12).
3. X2 traps in Sections A, B, and C.
4. X2 defends the weakside high post and horizontal passing lanes when the ball is trapped in Section D. X2 plays weakside positioning when traps occur in Sections E and F.

Rules for X3

1. X3 is your smallest and quickest defender. He is your small offensive forward.
2. X3 picks up the first attacker around the perimeter right of X1. X3 denies this man the ball until he sees X1 cut his man toward X3. Then X3 races hard to trap in Section D.
3. X3 also traps in Sections E and F.
4. X3 defends the passing lane into weakside high post and shades the horizontal passing lane when the ball is located in Section A. When the ball advances into Section B or C, X3 plays weakside defense.

Rules for X4

1. X4 is your second biggest and second quickest inside defender. He picks up any player in the middle lane. He goes out as far as the half-court line and as deep as the free throw line.

2. X4 plays whoever is high and in the middle lane. If no one is there, X4 covers the second attacker around the perimeter left or right of X1. If someone is located second to the left and another attacker stands second to the right of X1, X4 takes the second attacker to X1's right (this makes your defense appear to be a 1-2-2 trap).

3. X4 defends the strongside high post when the ball is trapped in Sections A or D.

4. X4 traps when the ball is passed into Sections B or E. If the ball is passed crosscourt from Section B to E or from Section E to B, the weakside wing, X2 or X3, must hold the new pass receiver until X4 can arrive.

5. X4 defends the low post when the ball rests in Sections C or F.

Rules for X5

1. X5 is your slowest defender, probably your center.

2. X5 picks up anyone who is located in a corner or either low-post position. If all five attackers come up higher than the free throw line, X5 takes the second attacker around the perimeter left of X1 (this puts the defense in a 2-3 alignment). When the ball is in Section A and X5 is covering a player high (say in Section B), the low post must be covered by X3. When the ball is in Section D and X3 guards a defender in Section E, X5 must cover the low-post position.

3. X5 defends both low-post positions when the ball is in Sections A or D, unless the match-up was in a 2-3. X5 shades the strongside low post, but he must be able to deflect any lob pass to the weakside low post.

4. With the ball in Sections B or E, X5 drops to cover the strongside low post.

5. A ball passed into either corner, Sections C or F, requires X5 to trap, denying any baseline drive.

General Rules

1. No passes must be allowed into the middle lane. Guards X1 and X2 pick up their men before half-court and turn the ball outside.

2. Should the ball reach the middle lane above the key, X1 or X2 must play the attacker one-on-one until he pushes the ball to the sideline.

3. A pass to the middle lane near the free throw line requires X4 to force the ball outside while X2 and X3 drop to help X5 on the baseline. X1 helps X4.

Let's explore the possibilities. If the offense attacks the defense from a 1-2-2 formation, the above rules cover the same slides as the 1-2-2 half-court trap (chapter 7), just exchange X4 and X5's positioning. If the attacking formation appears to be the 1-3-1, the defensive slides will be the same as those in chapter 7 on the 1-3-1 trap, again exchanging X4 and X5.

Diagram 8-12 shows a 2-1-2 man-to-man match-up becoming a half-court zone trap following the previous rules. These slides are basically the same as those in chapter 6.

As 1 drives across the time line, X1 pushes him outside (Diagram 8-12). X2 has 2, the first attacker left of X1; X3 covers the first attacker right of X1. X4 defends the middle lane; and because X4 is above the free throw line, X5 must cover 4.

X3 goes to help X1 trap; X4, X2, and X5 move to their respective assignments. X4 defends the high post and 5, but he also shades any habit pass from 1 to 3. X2 drops to help X4 around the high-post area, but he shades the horizontal pass back toward 2. X5 races to cover the low-post areas, including the lob pass crosscourt to 4 near the basket area.

If a pass occurs in backcourt from 1 to 2, the defense remains the same, just on the opposite side of the court. X2 forces 2 to drive. X5 comes to trap and X3 drops to cover the low-post positions. This would differ slightly from the rules we gave. Or you could require X2 to recover, activating the give-the-outside—take-it-away (see chapter 1), forcing 2 to pick up the dribble or drive to the inside. Now X1 helps X2 trap and everyone is back in their match-up rules: X3 helping X4 defend the high post with X3 shading the horizontal and X4 shading the vertical. X5, meanwhile, drops to defend his low-post positions.

9

How to Recover from Presses Into Standard Half-Court Defenses

Proper recovery makes your press. That principle alone allows your defenders to press with confidence, with abandonment, without fear of being beaten. When this axiom is intensely learned, your defenders will become a ball-hawking, thieving, rampaging band of reckless marauders.

Defenders must remain aggressive, not only when attacking the offense at full-court but when beaten by a quick pass or a sudden offensive move; they must learn *never* to give up. They must remain mentally aggressive even while retreating. They must adopt the attitude: "Retreat, hell—we are just advancing in the opposite direction!" Then, and only then, will they be in the best frame of mind to recover correctly.

Many offensive players will feel they have defeated the press when they have crossed the ten-second line with a numerical advantage. These players tend to become careless with their passes, their cuts. Because of this complacency, the retreating defenders should not only have a definite responsibility or a distinct area to protect in the frontcourt, but they must remain very alert to crosscourt passes and to inside cutting maneuvers. It should not matter to the defense if they steal the ball early or late in their presses. A deflected pass even at the end of the press aids the defense.

When every player has mastered the techniques of proper retreating (see the drills in chapter 1), the supposedly safe frontcourt pass will become easily intercepted, the cutter who moves to the ball will charge the proper positioned defender. The defense, though initially outnumbered, will frequently steal a pass, compel a turnover, or force the bad or hurried shot.

Individual defenders have two avenues of response to offensive teams who have burst through the press. Each player must know his slides and perform them diligently, skillfully; or each defender must possess remarkable basketball savvy or be willing to learn that necessary and often elusive basketball science.

You should first teach the safety skills (see three-on-three call, three-on-two-on-one, etc. in chapter 1). Each potential defender who might be assigned the safety's duties or the weakside responsibilities of your elected press or presses must learn how to contain and delay an offensive thrust when outnumbered. Then you move to training the retreating weakside defenders (see Diagrams 1-23 and 1-24). The defenders learn if they never give up they can move half the length of the court on a single nonpenetrating pass; and they quickly see they can, by proper retreating, deflect or intercept the second or the penetrating pass. After your individual performers have developed their skills sufficiently, you are ready to address the matters of proper team retreating (chapter 9).

RETREATING TO THE
TWO HALF-COURT DEFENSES

There are two basic types of half-court defenses: man-to-man and zone. When you are full-court zone pressing unsuccessfully, you will want to retreat back into your half-court defense. The same is true of your three-quarter court and your drop-back zone presses. If you are half-court trapping, you could continue to stay in that trap for that possession unless you have stunted into another defense (see chapter 10 for some ways to call these changes). Half-court traps are complete defenses within themselves and do not require changing to a man-to-man or a zone. You can change if you like. Each type of defense, the full-court zone press, the drop-back zone press, and the half-court trap, will be shown retreating into a man-to-man defense and into a zone defense. The man-to-man defense will suffice to demonstrate retreating to particular individuals; the zone defense will illustrate methods of retreating to particular areas. If your half-court defense is some combination of both, you can derive techniques to help you develop retreating patterns.

THREE WAYS OF RETREATING
TO MAN-TO-MAN

There exists a school of thought which proclaims you cannot zone press (either full-court or drop-back) and fall back into a man-to-man defense at half-court. But this school forgot to tell John Wooden, winner of ten NCAA titles at UCLA, or Denny Crum, Coach of the Louisville Cardinals, who also have won an NCAA national title, or a host of high school coaches who have mastered one of the following recovery methods.

Basically there are three ways to match-up man-to-man after full-court zone pressing: (1) All defenders can sink to the basket before coming out to get their man; (2) all defenders can be assigned retreat areas before using rules to locate an assignment; and (3) three defenders can pick up their men while two may have to switch. Each technique receives extensive treatment below, including a discussion of their strengths and their weaknesses.

(1) Defenders Sinking to the Basket Area Before Finding Their Man. This is the weakest, the least sound, of all the methods of picking up man-to-man after zone pressing. It is also the simplest and the easiest to teach.

To teach your defenders to adjust from the zone press to the man-to-man defense at half-court, you instruct each to race back into the painted area, the key, the 15-foot-by-12-foot rectangle. From there your defenders will defend the inside cutters even if these inside men are not their assignments before moving outside to pick up their own men. Talking is a must. A defender would make such comments as "33 is loose inside," telling whoever was assigned to 33 to pick up 33 quickly. Naturally the defender who made the statement would deny the pass to 33 until 33's assigned defender arrives. Then the communicator would point to his own assignment around the perimeter and proclaim: "I have 24." In this manner all defenders first deny the inside pass before picking up their own man. This makes the inside defense tougher, but it allows, all too often, the deadly perimeter jump shot. While hurrying to find their man, block-outs are missed, second and third shots result, nullifying any advantage gained from simplicity.

If you choose this method of retreating, you can tutor it by drills. You can line up all five defenders on one end of the floor in a manner that allows three to have to trail two or two to have to trail three. When you use two defenders ahead of three, you should have three attackers ahead of the other two offensive players (Diagram 9-1). Toss the ball to an attacker. The three offensive players fast-break against the two defenders. The two defenders try to force two passes so X3, X4, and X5 can recover for defense. Players 3 and 4 race hard to get into the offense.

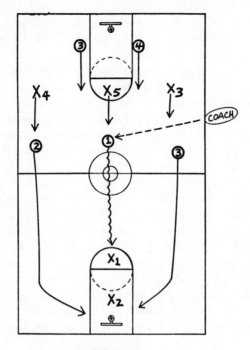

DIAGRAM 9-1

You make man-to-man assignments, and instruct your defenders to fall back into the key before coming outside to pick up their assignments.

This drill can be altered by allowing three defenders to be back against two attackers. Then have the other attackers and the other defenders race downcourt to score or to find their assignments.

Place five soon-to-be attackers around the basket with three assigned to their defensive boards and two guards to act as outlet pass receivers. Have three attackers soon-to-be defenders go to their offensive boards, and two of the attackers soon-to-be defenders back to defend against the fast-break. Toss the ball on the backboard. If the offense gets the ball, they put it back in the basket. If the defense gets the rebound, they outlet pass and fast-break. Now all attackers and defenders race down the floor: the defense to pick up man-to-man and the offense to score as quickly as possible. This is a multipurpose drill. Not only do your defenders learn to pick up man-to-man but they must stop a fast-break. The offense is getting work on their break. This picking up man-to-man simulates the type of pickups that are involved in stopping a team that has burst through the press.

(2) Assign Retreat Area Before Applying Rules for Picking Up. Because most opponent's systems are consistent from their opening day of practice until their final game and because scouting has long ago become an art, assigning areas of coverage for your retreating defenders may be the best means of converting from a zone press into a man-to-man defense. A few simple rules will allow your defenders always to find their assigned men.

All trap and lane assignments take one of two forms, depending on your particular belief of zone pressing (Diagrams 9-2 and 9-3). Diagram 9-2 shows popular two trappers, two gap shooters, and a safety. Diagram 9-3 depicts the less popular two trappers, one rover and two safety.

Regardless of which trap or press you prefer, they all begin in one of these two alignments. In both diagrams the arrows illustrate a retreat route into a 2-3 zone before picking up man-to-man. You might prefer to retreat to a 1-2-2 or a 1-3-1 before reverting to your man-to-man coverage. You should choose the same retreat pattern as your basic zone defense for that year. That simplifies matters for your defenders. You could, if you prefer, have your defenders retreat into the alignment your opponents will use to attack your man-to-man defense. This last method requires changing retreat patterns from game to game.

Your scouting reports should tell you where the opponents will line up to begin their man-to-man offense if their attack against your press fails to get them a quick basket. Your rules for picking up should correspond as closely as possible with the assignments you prefer for that

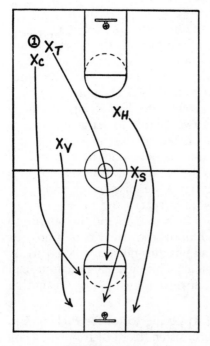

DIAGRAM 9-2

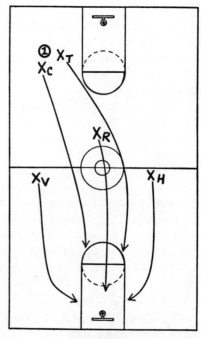

DIAGRAM 9-3

particular game. However, do not adjust too much or you will confuse your defenders. It is better to have a standard retreat, one practiced all season long and thereby perfected, and let the offense see if they can break it, than to change drastically from game to game. Therein lies the major weakness of this method of retreat: you may terminate in assignments each possession which you do not prefer, sometimes detrimental to your team defense.

The rules are simple. Each defender retreats to his assigned area picking up the attacker in his area. If there are no attackers in a particular area, this defender guards the basket area until he can spot the area where two offensive men are. All defenders must be taught to point to and call out the number of the man they are covering: "I've got 12" is a proper response. This enables the defender without a man to locate his "assignment" quickly.

The whole method is probably the best drill to teach this type coverage. You can either make it live, using your next opponent's offense or using a free-lance attack; or you can keep a structured control scrimmage by allowing 1 to pass out of the trap set in Diagram 9-2 or Diagram 9-3. Once this pass is completed, instruct the receiver to attack the basket or to advance the ball into frontcourt before setting into an offensive formation to attack a man-to-man half-court defense.

(3) Three Defenders Pick Up Their Men While Two May Switch. This is easily the best method of retreating from a zone press into a man-to-man half-court defense. It permits greater defensive pressure even when the ball advances into the scoring area. It allows the defenders to stay matched with their pregame assignments eliminating any possible mismatch, except possibly between the two adjusting defenders. And it is very simple to teach. It is no more difficult than a simple "switch" when playing half-court man-to-man exclusively. Its sole weakness: For a few possible moments there could be, does not have to be, a mismatch. Even when a mismatch does occur, the two defenders involved can trade men as soon as their men appear on the weak side or when they come close together.

The rules for this coverage are as simple as the pregame assignment list. Each defender picks up his originally assigned man. That's it, with one exception: If the safety (or the weakside defender) must stop the advancement of the ball, he yells out the number of his assigned man. This tells the safety's teammate (or weakside defender's teammate) who was originally assigned the man with the ball the number he is to cover. This means that the defenders will always have their assignments, will always be matched with the attacker you want them to have; and maybe the safety (or weakside defender) and one other defender will have traded assignments. They trade back as quickly as the two congregate without either having the ball or when the ball moves to a point where both attackers are on the weak side.

Drills can be created to teach this coverage from three-on-three to five-on-five. The best approach is the whole (five-on-five) method. It can be done from a live scrimmage situation, using the next opponent's offense or a free-lance attack; or it can be done from a controlled, structured scrimmage. The latter is superior. From Diagrams 9-2 and 9-3, allow 1 to pass out of the trap. The new receiver pushes the ball upcourt, attacking before the zone press can recover. This forces the safety to stop the ball and the weak side to cover the basket area (see the tandem drill in chapter 1). A pass to another attacker requires the weakside defender to stop the shot or continued penetration (see the safety drills in chapter 1). By this time all the defenders should have recovered and picked up their man, with the possible exception of the weakside defender, the bottom man on the tandem defense (see chapter 1). If he has his assignment, he yells out the number of the attacker originally assigned to him before the game. This tells the man who should be guarding the ball handler to get the communicated number. For example, let's say these were the pregame assignments: Defender A has 10, B has 12, C has 24, D has 44, and E has 55. Player 24 has received the pass and is driving toward the goal but D picks him up, stopping further penetration. D yells "44." This tells C to pick up "44." So A has 10, B has 12, C has 44, D has 24, and E chases 55. Whenever possible C and D will trade back.

HALF-COURT TRAPS INTO MAN-TO-MAN COVERAGE

All three of the previous coverages work against the full-court press, the three-quarter court zone press, and the drop-back zone press. But the half-court trap must remain in the half-court trap, change to the basic zone of the trap, or stunt into man-to-man coverage. Any of the stunts and techniques described in chapter 1 can be used as the key to switch the half-court trap into a man-to-man defense. Of course, these same stunts can keep the defense in the original half-court trap (for keys to calling these see chapter 10). It can also be used at the full-court zone press level (see chapter 10).

Diagram 9-4 shows the give-the-outside—take-it-away stunt used from the 1-2-2 half-court trap formation. X1 gives 1 the outside but forces 1 to reverse at a predetermined spot. X3 knows this is about to occur. X3 races over to clamp a trap on 1. A key word sends X1 to cover 3. X2 meanwhile dropped to decoy 1 and to cover 2. X4 guards 4, and X5 finds 5. If 1 holds the ball for five seconds, it is a violation. If 1 makes a bad pass, the defense can get a fast-break basket. If 1 successfully finds a teammate, the defense uses the give-the-outside—take-it-away stunt to go from the half-court trap to the man-to-man defense.

DIAGRAM 9-4

The defense could have used a different code word to signal the defenders to stay in their half-court trap. This would have required X3 to become the new point guard, and X1 to assume the duties of a wing. In other words X1 and X3 just exchanged duties and responsibilities.

Of course, the three coverages discussed in the previous section that enabled the defense to change from the full-court, three-quarter court, and the drop-back zone presses into man-to-man will work for the half-court trap. The drawback to using them is your half-court trap can execute only one trap without confusing your defense. You can trap as the ball comes into frontcourt, then use one of the three previously mentioned coverages to change to man-to-man. Many professional teams are beginning to use this technique very successfully.

WAYS OF RETREATING INTO A ZONE

Diagrams 9-2 and 9-3 demonstrate the retreat into a 2-3 or 2-1-2 zone from the two full-court trapping situations. Other retreat routes could be mapped for each defender if these are not compatible with your belief. Change the routes to correspond with the skills of your personnel.

For example, suppose you wanted XH to be your defensive center and XS to be your defensive forward in Diagram 9-2. You would merely reroute those two retreat patterns. Diagrams 9-5 and 9-6 display the retreat routes into a 1-3-1 zone, and Diagrams 9-7 and 9-8 show the retreats into a basic 1-2-2 zone.

Retreat patterns into zone defenses from full-court zone presses will work from almost any route you diagram. The two important ingredients: (1) You drill on them and drill on them and drill on them; and (2) you fix the routes to get the maximum out of your material. It is not difficult to retreat from a zone press into a zone defense.

Diagram 9-5 depicts the basic recovery pattern from the two traps, two gap shooters, and a safety alignment into the 1-3-1 zone defense at half-court. One trapper, XT, takes the point; the other trapper, XC, takes the wing. XH also retreats to a wing. If the ball had been on the other side of the court, XH and XC would still retreat to the wings. XV takes the deep baseline position; XS takes the high-post defensive position.

Diagram 9-6 illustrates the retreating routes from the two trap, one rover, and two safety defensive pressing scheme into the 1-3-1 zone at half-court. XC and XR race into the wing positions. They would also

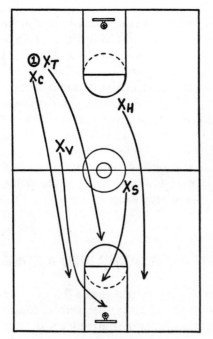
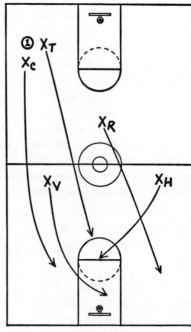

DIAGRAM 9-5   DIAGRAM 9-6

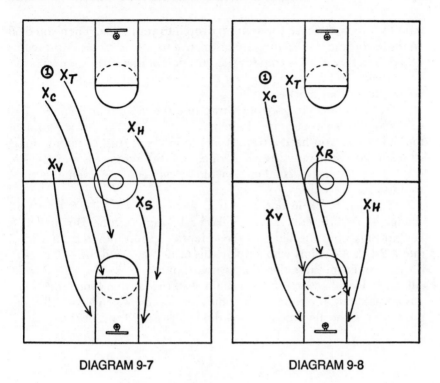

DIAGRAM 9-7   DIAGRAM 9-8

have the same responsibilities in the press, but on opposite sides of the court. XT retreats to the point; XH, one of the safeties, takes the high post; and XV becomes the baseline defender.

Diagram 9-7 shows the standard retreat route from the two trapper, two gap shooters, one safety scheme into the 1-2-2 zone at the half-court level. XT takes the point. XC and XH have similar duties in the press, and they retreat to the wing positions of the 1-2-2 zone. XV and XS have identical press duties, and they retreat to the two back positions of the 1-2-2 half-court basic zone.

Diagram 9-8 shows the 1-2-2 zone from the two trappers, one rover, two safeties defensive pressing alignment. XT again goes to the point. XC and XR have identical press duties, and they become the wings of the 1-2-2 zone. XV and XH, the two safeties, have similar responsibilities while pressing, and they have exactly the same duties when retreating to the 1-2-2 zone defense, namely baseline deep defenders.

HALF-COURT TRAPS INTO ZONE COVERAGES

Going from half-court traps into a basic zone coverage is not only safe but very easy to accomplish. As coach, you determine where you want to trap and where you want to drop into your zone. Then you drill on these coverages until they are instinctive to your athletes. Most teams who do not stay in their trap for the duration of that possession will trap only outside and then drop to their zone coverage on any pass completed below the 28-foot marker.

Teaching how to go from a trap into the basic zone belongs in all teams' defensive repertoire. It helps the trap to take on a plural or multiple look. You have a trap, stunts to go from trap to man-to-man, stunts to go from trap to regular zone, and different areas and times to trap. This defensive combination alone can confuse even the most sophisticated offense.

You can begin in one zone trap formation, say a 1-2-2 trap, and change it to a different type zone, like a 2-1-2 regular zone. Do this with a key, and map out the slides so the defensive group moves from a 1-2-2 into a 2-1-2. All teams who employ this tactic wait until the ball goes to the corner. From there the zone, if not trapping, looks like a 2-1-2 zone. All zones look like a 2-1-2 with the ball in the corner. Once the ball is passed back out, the zone can become any alignment you want. All zones go to their basic alignments when the ball is passed out of the corner.

10

How to Improve Your
Zone Pressuring System

Zone pressuring as a seasonal plan can be excitingly creative. It can take the form of one zone press run the same way over and over again; or it can take a myriad of forms. Several zone presses run at different times or under different situations, a mixture of zone press slides, a stunt or two from one or more zone presses are but a few examples. The opportunities are limitless.

Any way you figure it there will be those nights when you have to come up with something different if you are to win. You will not have your opponent's individual skills. You must rely on other factors if you are to win. A zone press can be the great equalizer, but to zone press your team must be in excellent shape, physically and mentally. Fatigue impairs athletic skills and shortens desire. Good pressing teams can cause an opponent to fatigue, and that conditioning can permit a lesser skilled team to defeat a more talented club.

Psychological conditioning of defenders is as important as physical conditioning. The full-court zone press used as a basic part of your game plan has a much better chance of being successful than if you use it only as a desperation or catch-up tactic. Your team will execute better when they are close or ahead than if you wait until the closing seconds of a lost game. Plus, if you run your zone press or combination of zone presses, from opening tip to final buzzer, your opponents will become fatigued earlier, lessening their desire to win. They often become mentally as well as physically fatigued.

But which zone press? Or maybe more than one? Or even a system of zone presses and stunts? You will pick your five best players based on their basketball abilities. Before practice begins, you will have little or no idea of their aggregate size, speed, quickness, etc. Regardless of their limitations or assets, there is a zone press for you. Evaluate your material, study the zone press options that will be best for your evaluated material, determine what you want from your zone press, and choose that zone press or combination of presses and stunts. All those concepts have been offered in chapters 1 through 9. This chapter will help you determine where to use your presses, when to use them, and what combination of signals are available.

WHAT TYPE OF PRESSURE TO USE

Know Yourself. This above all else: To thine own self be true! In coaching basketball, this maxim must be obeyed. No coach can win unless he teaches only what he believes. Players immediately recognize when a coach is being untrue to himself. They don't learn as well, and they will not perform as intensely.

Zone pressing by nature is a calculated gamble. How much of a gamble depends on your nature, your aggressiveness, your evaluation of your personnel's physiological and psychological make-up, and defensive slides and stunts you choose from this text.

Know Your Personnel. Zone presses do not require each member to be proficient at all phases of defense. Some may specialize. In man-to-man presses, all defenders must cover the spectrum of good defensive play. It is possible to operate an effective zone press with players of lesser defensive abilities. Of course, your zone press would operate best with five top-notch defenders.

The greater your team speed, the larger the area of the court your defense may be extended. For teams with great overall speed, the full-court press is your answer. For teams with no speed, one-quarter court may be small enough to get you beat. The great majority of teams lie somewhere between these two extremes.

Know Your Presses. To know a zone press, you must realize what personnel will run it best. Then the slides and traps become important.

After you have determined the best zone press for your unique blend of players, you must decide if you want three traps, two traps, or one trap. Your fears and aggressive thinking will determine how many traps you want from your press—this does not include the short throwbacks. After you have decided how many traps you want, determine where on the court you want the first trap to occur.

Then, decide on the slides that best suit your personnel. You can even run two sets of slides if it matches your personality and if it will not confuse your athletes. Next you add your stunts.

Before you decide on tempo, you should decide what you want from your press. Your objectives will help determine your tempo. You can grind it out from beginning to end by playing it conservatively, and then gamble to steals at the moment the offense indicates stealing is available. Alternating "off" and "on" can be an example of playing it conservatively; stunts and aggressive trapping techniques from three trapping areas easily force offensive misaction.

Multiple Defenses or Single Press. How many different presses, stunts, and traps your players can absorb becomes the basic question. Your own beliefs, of course, will place limits on what you teach. You have many paths you can take: you can have one press and use only one trap with no stunts; you can teach one press, using alternate slides with many traps and stunts; or you can tutor several different alignments, mixing in different slides, traps, and stunts. You can be as complex in a single press as you want; or you can be as simple in a set of multiple presses as you desire.

Half-court zone coaches would never consider entering a game with only one zone. The same should hold true for full-court zones. This does not mean you have to have a 1-2-2, a 2-2-1, and a 2-1-2. You can stay in the same formation but just expand and contract, stunt, or go "off" and "on." You can teach only a few fundamental moves and use these same techniques from several different alignments.

Many coaches think quickness is a necessity for pressing. But in a lot of cases, thinking quick will compensate for not being quick. Whatever you give your athletes should not be so much that you confuse them. Drill until the methods are instinctive. For every single two-men strongside offensive play, there are multiple defensive coverages available: "flick," "hedge," "jump," "trap," play-it straight, etc. You can thoroughly confuse any dribbler by alternating these natural and instinctive coverages without teaching other stunts or slides.

Some offensive teams attack off-front zone presses one way and even-front zone presses another way. Some teams attack one type of alignment better than they do the other. When either of those two offensive developments occur, you should be willing to change alignments. You can run the same stunt or team technique, but just the show of a different zone front can impel the offensive team into a weaker attack. Frequently changing defensive formations will confuse even the best attacking teams into a few early mistakes.

Stunting also compels offensive mistakes. In fact, stunting leads to two offensive conditions. The attackers overreact thinking a trap off the regular press is going to occur. They quickly make the habit pass, the pass your interceptor has been waiting for, the pass you drilled your team to expect. Or the offense becomes overcautious, hesitating to make the pass, again fearing the regular trap or slides. This offensive reaction also enables the interceptor to gain an advantageous position for the interception, deflection.

If you choose to go with a single press, you must decide how deep you will teach it, how complicated to make it. You choose your trap areas, stunts, slides, places, and pace. If you choose to go multiple formation, you decide how many. Then choose the different combinations you want. You can choose different ones for each press, or you can use the same techniques in each different press formation. Multiple or single and how complicated is your first major decision in developing your zone pressing system.

WHERE AND WHEN TO TRAP

Where and when to trap requires considering two sets of facts: Your own personnel and your opponent's personnel. From your evaluation of your personnel, you develop your seasonal plans. Decide on your press or presses, your stunts, the number of traps, your slides, and all the other little decisions that makes your press work. From your study of your opponents, you develop that night's game plan.

Because of the wide variation in skills of your opponents for the year, it is best if you teach all three trapping areas in each of your presses (Diagram 10-1). This does not include the short throwbacks. Because of these variations in skills, it pays to have a full-court zone press, a dropback press, and a half-court trap. You never know which teams on your schedule are quicker than you. You never know which press your individual opponents will not be able to attack successfully. Each defensive stunt that you teach will work effectively regardless of the press you are using.

In deciding on a game plan, if you have a mixture of presses, stunts, and initial trapping areas available, you have a better chance for victory. We advocate teaching all three downcourt traps (Diagram 10-1) for your full-court press, and we favor having these available on both sides of the court. This means you do not have only the three downcourt areas covered, but you also have worked out a means of covering long and short throwback passes. When you play a quicker opponent, you merely tell your defenders not to trap in Area 1, but to begin the trap in Area 2 (Diagram 10-1). When playing a weaker opponent, someone you should beat easily, begin your trap in Area 1. Keep the pressure on the entire game.

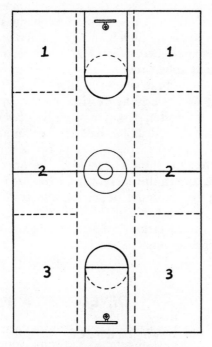

DIAGRAM 10-1

If you also have a half-court trap with different slides from your full-court zone press, you are ready to pull off some major upsets. If you also have prepared yet another set of traps and slides for the shooting area, you will prove almost unbeatable.

Now all you have to do is consider the times you want to apply each press, each trap, each stunt. Your guiding postulate should be: NEVER LET YOUR OPPONENT'S OFFENSE ADJUST TO YOUR DEFENSE. When you feel they have figured out an attack to defeat your press with poise, switch to your next press or trap. Keep their attack off-balance. This is a tricky decision. You never want to leave a press, a trap, or a stunt too early, but you definitely never want to leave it too late. When your opponents gain confidence in their attack against your press, it spreads enthusiasm and momentum to them. We have found it is better to leave too early than too late. You can always come back later.

Sometimes a press is not working for you early. You should discard it. Later in that same game when you come back to it, it may be a tremendous game saver for you.

Whenever mighty-momentum is on your side, press, press, press! You can gain several quick turnovers and scores in a row. Teach your players to be ultra-aggressive in this period, but also recognize quickly when your opponents start to break that mighty-momentum. Sometimes one offensive breakthrough for an easy score changes things, but most always it takes more than one such basket. You will recognize, after a few years of coaching experience, when the other team has thoroughly solved your particular zone press.

There is always one time when you should train your defenders to become extra alert and overly aggressive. As the count in backcourt nears ten seconds, panic often strikes in offensive players, no matter how experienced they are. The dribbler–ball handler knows he must hurry. He quickly tries to dribble through a trap, or he attempts a hurried unwise pass. All defenders should be taught to become more alert, more active as the ball remains in the backcourt for five seconds. Gap shooters should be told that even a finger deflection may result in a turnover. A clean interception is rare, but a slight deflection is possible on almost every pass. A ball off its target, rolling free, belongs as much to the defense as to the offense—maybe more.

DEVELOPING A SIGNAL SYSTEM

To call a time-out to switch a defense or to call a defensive stunt is an inexcusable waste of a precious time-out. There are just too many acceptable means of communicating such defensive switches to merit using the time-out.

Regardless of whether you intend to use the multiple formations in your pressing system or to use only one defense but do several things out of it, you will need a signaling system. First, there must be communication between the bench and the floor; then there must be no mistakes made in the communication among the players on the floor.

Communication from the bench to the floor is relatively easy. It can take one of three forms: It can occur as the game progresses, it can already have been set and predrilled, or it can be a combination of the two.

If signaling is to occur as the game progresses, you want to signal the entire five or tell only one player and let him tell the other four. Signals are frequently missed when you deal with more than one defender. We advocate letting the defensive quarterback relay the messages to the other four. There are many ways you can get your message to your defensive coordinator. You can use a hand signal, you can use your voice, you can use color schemes on cards or towels. Use these methods when there is a lull in the action: at the free throw line, during jump balls, or after a violation. Or you can use these methods as the game continues. Position your bench where your defensive expert always spots you as he retreats after each offensive possession.

There are three major ways this defensive coordinator can relay your message to the other four. He can tell them when there is a lull in the action, like a huddle at the free throw line. This will not automatically occur. You must drill on it during practice. A second acceptable method is to require all defenders to look at the defensive quarterback after each offensive possession. This defensive signal-caller holds up a certain number of fingers to indicate the defense for that trip or successive trips down the floor. When using this method, it might be advantageous to design a spot for the defensive signal-caller—for example, the center circle or the defensive free throw key. A third method of switching defenses begins with the court location of the defensive quarterback (Diagram 10-2). Diagram 10-2 demonstrates five different spots for the defensive quarterback to locate. The other four defenders must look in the center lane to find their defensive quarterback. At the one position, all defenders play their designated full-court press. If you have more than one press or if you intend to stunt, you can further complicate the defense and confuse the offense by a hand signal. Of course, this technique is available at all the five spots. Spot number two means a three-quarter court press. Spot number three tells the defense you are in your drop-back press. Four indicates a half-court trap. Five illustrates your basket protecting zone or man-to-man defense.

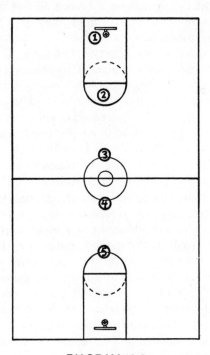

DIAGRAM 10-2

Defenses can be called by planning every game situation. There is a team in our league, for example, which goes to a 1-2-1-1 zone press on made baskets from the field. They show a 2-2-1 zone press on all made free throws. They man-to-man face-guard press on all violations whether the offensive team inbounds the ball on the sidelines or the baseline. On all misses from the free throw line or from the field, they drop back into their man-to-man at half-court. On made free throws, they run a 2-1-2 zone at their basket area, and on made baskets they drop into a 1-3-1 zone. This rigid planning allows the opponents to prepare an advance plan. They also know your signals. Of course, your opponents would have only a few days preparation and you would have had the entire season. You would still be better prepared.

Another excellent approach to game situation signaling is by score or time. When your score is odd, run a 1-2-1-1 press into a man-to-man. When your score is even, run a 2-2-1 press into a half-court zone. When you miss, drop back into a half-court trap. This same method is available by using the time clock. On odd minutes you run the 1-2-1-1 into a man-to-man. On even minutes you press 2-2-1 into a zone. On all misses you retreat into your half-court trap.

There is another approach that defies scouts from checking your keys and planning and drilling their offenses for your defenses. It is called situational change-ups. Let's say you have five defenses or stunts you intend to teach this year. You number them in order 41, 42, 43, 44, and 45. You run 41 until a key situation occurs, say a called violation— walking, palming, three seconds, five seconds, etc. This situation automatically puts you into your 42 plan. This continues throughout the entire game.

This process opens up even more avenues. You could change your order, such as 41, 43, 45, 42, 44. You could change the key to a made free throw. One made free throw would move you from 41 to 42. If you made two you would move two notches from 41 to 42 to 43. In case a defender got confused you could have a voice command to get him back on cue. Your key could even be any change of possession of the basketball. Every time you scored the defense would change, but the defense would also change when you committed a violation.

Of course, you could combine the two major methods of communication; calling the signals as the game progresses or having preset and predrilled signals. For example, use your preset, predrilled signals the first three and one-half quarters and then change to calling from the bench for the last half of a quarter. This would allow you to make corrections and adjustments for what would help your team the best during the last and often the most important part of the game.

If you have exceptionally smart basketball players, you can have a set of situational signals for when you are ahead and another set for when you are behind. You could activate these early in the ball game or late in the fourth quarter. This would allow you to gamble more when you had to have the ball and play it conservatively when you were ahead. This type of thinking also allows for preplanning and predrilling. All too often keys are missed by one or more defenders in crucial situations. By having a preset, predrilled signal system for when you are ahead and having a different set for when you are behind you would eliminate some of those missed signals.

When you want to switch from one defense to another in midaction of any particular possession, like going from zone to man-to-man, there is a signal system available for you. You can accomplish this by a code word or by using predrilled stunts. For example, you could let a code word such as "home" mean zone and "break" mean man-to-man. Suppose you are trapping in your 1-2-2 full-court zone press when your opponents toss the ball crosscourt to a short throwback position. Upon receiving the throwback pass, the defender responsible for containment yells "break." Each defender repeats it. The defense switches from zone to man-to-man. This type signal system is very dangerous, but it can also be most productive. Another way to affect the same switch from zone to man-to-man would be simply to rule: On all throwback passes the zone press changes to man-to-man.

This signal system, in fact, is available for all stunts. You must decide which stunt you want to call which defense. You could rule, for example, any time you run-and-jump, give-the-outside—then-take-it-away, or peel-down you will switch from zone coverage to man-to-man. Any time you run-and-jump "trap," cover throwbacks, and force the reverse dribble you will stay zone. This signal system is workable only if all five of your defenders can read what your defense is trying to accomplish and what stunt you have called.

Each of these signal systems can be modified to only one defense, say a 1-2-1-1 press, a 1-2-2 drop-back, and a 1-2-2 half-court trap. They also work even if you choose to use several defenses but only in a particular spot: You are going to half-court trap, but you want to use the 1-3-1 trap, the 1-2-1-1 trap, and the 2-1-2 trap.

By no means have we covered all possible signal systems. What we have given, however, should suffice to allow you to create the one you can live with.

KNOW METHODS OF ATTACK SO YOU CAN ADJUST YOUR PRESS

There are many types of zone press attacks, but all full-court zone press offenses incorporate certain basic elements. These basic elements can be broken into three categories: the lane of attack, the method of attack, and the number of attackers.

Flashing and posting, a dribble and split game, the short pass attack, and the long pass attack illustrate the method of attack. These can be incorporated into a free movement or they can become part of a patterned attack. Sideline offenses can attack with only one extra clever dribbler or they can bring down their entire five to try to outnumber the defenders.

The defense does not have to be at the mercy of the offense. Instead of reacting to whatever mode of attack your opponents decide upon, you can force them to play your game. By proper evaluation of your scouting reports, you should know your opponent's system of attacking presses. Wherever they decide to attack, you can impel them to attack elsewhere. To do this, you must know as much about zone presses as possible. Your primary objective is to compel the offense into an attack they have not practiced. If they want to attack down the sidelines, make them move down the middle lane. If they want to use two men to attack in backcourt, make them bring down a third. If they want to dribble, make them use some form of passing game.

Some coaches choose to have a player flash into the middle lane for a pass. If the pass does not occur momentarily, this flash pivot attacker begins to post, trying to get the defender on his back, waiting for the penetrating pass. Any time the pass comes to this player, he immediately pivots to check downcourt for another poster in the middle lane, or he looks to the opposite side lane from whence the ball entered.

To defense this attack, you should exaggerate a slough into the middle lane. Not only does this give your defense good positioning to deny the flash cutter the ball on his initial cut, but it frequently forces the lob pass into the off-ball lane. This is a difficult pass for the offense to complete and an easy one for the defense to intercept.

Many coaches believe that the best offense against a zone press is the short passing attack. They may want to go down the sideline, down the middle, or a combination of the two. Teams that advance the ball with a series of short passes must be defensed in a manner that encourages the dribble or the long pass. This takes them out of their game and into the jaws of the zone defense.

Other coaches prefer to use the overhead two-handed long pass or to use the baseball pass. But long passes frequently get away from the passer or are fumbled by the receiver. Almost all zone presses drill daily on interception of these long errant passes.

With so many expert ball handlers around some coaches like to dribble against the full-court zone press. When a double-team trap approaches the talented dribbler, this penetrator splits the two defenders either with a clever dribbling maneuver or he leaps into the air and passes to a teammate. This used to be taboo offensively, but with the expert ball handlers growing in number daily is it as safe an attack as any other.

How do you stop the dribble and split attack? You work extremely hard on your double-teaming techniques. If the driver-passer is so skilled that he breaks tight double-teams consistently, then you must employ the loose double-team or you must drop your traps nearer the basket area.

Patterned offenses offer the poorest choice to the offensive coach. Two or three patterns are easily scouted and easily defended. After a few runnings in the first quarter, the defense adjusts and the patterns become ineffective. A large number of patterns would make the attack too complicated even for the offensive players to learn much less execute.

Some offensive-minded coaches believe it best to break a press by passing down the sidelines. They reason that deflections would go out-of-bounds, that interceptions would be fewer because the interceptor would touch the sideline as he intercepted the ball, and that completions would break the press.

It is more difficult for a moving defender to intercept a pass going down the outside lanes because his momentum will carry him out-of-bounds. But it is also easier for the defender to deny vertical passing attacks. As defensive coach, you want to deny the sideline penetration if that is the offensive preference.

Coaches who prefer to attack the middle lane reason they have more passing avenues available from the middle. They reason that all those passing lanes from the middle cannot be covered by only five defenders. They tell their players to post or flash into the middle lane, receive the ball, check downcourt in the middle lane, then check the outside lane opposite the entry pass.

Sagging the off-ball defender clogs the middle, and you must keep the ball out of the middle. You want to force the lob pass into the lane opposite where the ball is located. This is a difficult pass to complete and a very easy one to intercept. Your next favorite location of the pass to be directed is down the sidelines.

Not only do you want to dictate what offensive technique you will allow and the lane where you will allow it, but you want to compel the attackers to use a different number of players from what they practiced. If your opponents bring only one guard downfloor to receive the inbounds pass and then to attack your press with that guard and the player who tossed the ball inbounds, then face-guard or shortstop this lone guard. This forces the offense to bring down another player. If they decide to attack your press with three players downcourt, allow the inbounds pass and trap it. Put your other two defenders in the gap between the passer and his two teammate receivers. The offense must reply with a fourth attacker. Make the offense use the numbers they have not practiced and/or the numbers you want them to use.

ADJUSTMENTS

Adjustments can come in an infinite variety of forms, but they affect your program in only two areas: adjustments for that one particular game, or adjustments in the seasonal plans. To adjust during a game you need to understand your presses, your stunts, and what your opponents are attempting to accomplish. These adjustments can be preplanned and predrilled. For example, the peel-down stunt leaves an area open that would be closed by the give-the-outside—take-it-away stunt. When your opponents find a soft spot, it is your job to know how to close it, even when you plan showing them a soft spot before eliminating it.

Adjusting a game plan usually occurs in hectic moments under stressful conditions. To adjust your seasonal pressing plans you can take a long leisurely and calculated look at what your presses have been accomplishing. If some part is not functioning as well as the whole, then consider discarding it. To discard it, you need not tell your players. That might cause a loss of confidence in the whole defensive system. Simply phase-out practicing it. To add something new requires much deeper considerations. Too often coaches see something at a clinic or read something in an article or a book and fall in love with it. Before you consider such a move, make sure you need the addition. If possible, add it to an existing plan instead of creating something entirely new. Make sure it is perfect for your personnel. Otherwise it will not provide you with the results you anticipated.

Adjustments in your seasonal program could be in strategy. For example, you could have been running a regular 2-2-1 zone press after made field goals. You ran a 2-2-1 with immediate traps after made free throws. Now switch these two assignments. Add: On all throwbacks switch the zone press to a man-to-man press. Now you have changed your strategy for the remainder of the year, but you have taught nothing new if you already had a man-to-man press.

An adjustment that frequently works but can open up much criticism for you is to run one press until tournament time and then change to a complementary press. This new press should differ only slightly from your original press. A few ways to effect this change: switch the alignment but keep all your stunts and traps; keep your alignment but change some of your stunts and slides; extend your original press to another area of the court—for example, take your 1-2-2 full-court zone press and make it into a 1-2-2 half-court trap. You keep the same slides, so really you are learning very little new. But your opponents must prepare anew for you. You have gained an advantage in strategy and in preparation.

Not only can you change your press on a seasonal basis, but strategies also play an important part in victory or defeat of any ball game. First among strategies is the development of a proper tempo. You must never allow the opponent to adjust to your defensive tempo. When you get the "feeling" of offensive adjustment, you should change the pace of your defensive pressure. This will create violations, turnovers, and interceptions. But this will be the trickiest of your bench-coaching decisions. You should never leave your press too soon. It may take a few possessions after a change for your team to adapt to the offensive mode of attack. Yet offensive teams will solve any press eventually, so you must know when to leave, change to a new one, change the pace (from "on" to "off," for example), or change from one stunt to another. Remember: Once you leave your press do not be afraid to resume it at a later time in the game. Often when you resume it, it works with great effectiveness. Too many coaches never return to their press during any game once the opposing teams show they can defeat it. Have courage.

When your press is working and the opposing coach calls a time-out, leave your press for a few possessions. The opposing coach called the time-out to instruct his team on methods of beating your press. A few possessions later, the opposing players will not work their coach's strategy. They will have collectively forgotten their coach's instruction, so reactivate your press.

The simplest of all adjustments—and there are many during any game—is to trap further downcourt or to trap nearer the basket. The offensive attack that works well against the 1-2-2 full-court zone press will not work well against the 1-2-2 drop-back. What is successful against the drop-back will not succeed against the 1-2-2 half-court trap. The defense learned only one set of slides, one group of stunts, and extend and contract, but the attackers must have three different offenses to be successful.

Some teams will dribble and split against your full-court press. You should drop back to your half-court trap. Now if a team dribbles against you, it will help your weakside defense. Some teams will be successful against odd front presses but they fold when faced with an even front press and vice versa. You can even compel teams to play your game by showing them an open passing lane, preferably one not included in their planned attack, one practiced daily, before closing it with an alternate stunt.

Game strategies take on a myriad of forms. The more you know about presses, the better you understand your personnel. The more experience you gain in evaluating your opponent's method of attacking, the easier it will be for you always to make the correct game adjustment.

You should also use the rule book during any game. Don't let your opponents get the ball in quickly after you score, especially late in a game you are losing. Call a time-out after you make a basket. You can have your players come to the bench or you can request that the official continue the game. You can call the time-out to set up your face-guard zone press and never allow your opponent's players to go near their bench. You can also have a substitute ready to enter the game on any thrown away ball or after a made free throw. Use your time-out wisely in late game situations.

If you really have courage you might consider this tempo strategy. Make a scientific ball-control team run, especially if your team is faster. Make a great running ball club run out of control by applying more and more defensive pressure.

THE STUFF LEGENDS ARE MADE OF

More than two decades ago I attended a basketball coaching clinic at the University of Tennessee. Big-named college coaches were on the podium elaborating on their particular philosophies and techniques. Lesser known but equally enthusiastic basketball minds fanatically copied word for word and diagram for diagram in hopes of someday being like "them."

I knew almost all of the three or four hundred who attended those crisp autumn sessions on basketball. Some have since quit coaching and gone into other fields for untold reasons. Others have moved up to become in a small measure like "them." A few remain where they were.

Stories still circulate on two who attended, listened, studied, dissimulated, and responded. Some of their accomplishments during their careers, I contend, simply cannot be true. They border on the super. I fear their accomplishments now have been intertangled with tall tales which continue to grow.

Technically one went in one direction; the other did not follow. One runs only one defense with multiple options; the other runs a multiple defense, each with only a few options. Yet both have been ultra-successful, both were legendary high school coaches while they were still in their thirties.

Those two dreamed their own dreams. Those two took out of all they heard only the portion they could use, discarding momentarily the rest, but remembering it for a later day. Those two did their own thinking, for long ago they realized they would settle for nothing less.

Those two now stand on podiums, delivering their own brand of basketball, hoping those who hear will measure what is said, will interpret it for their own program's needs. Two decades from now where will they be? What will people say? What do *you* think?

Index